This Book is For You

HOW TO FIND YOUR PASSION & PURPOSE
FROM THE MOTHER OF AN ABDUCTED CHILD

Marie White

ZAMIZ PRESS

Copyright © 2018 Marie White

Categories: NON-FICTION > SELF HELP > HAPPINESS
CHRISTIAN BOOKS & BIBLES > CHRISTIAN LIVING > SELF HELP

Unless otherwise noted, Scriptures are taken from THE HOLY BIBLE, NEW INTERNATIONAL VERSION®, NIV® Copyright © 1973, 1978, 1984, 2011 by Biblica, Inc.® Used by permission. All rights reserved worldwide. Copyrights continued on page 151.

The information in this book is not intended to replace the advice of a physician. It is for informational purposes only and any supplement, diet, or exercise program should be started under the advisement of a physician. Author and publisher are not responsible.

All rights reserved. No part of this publication may be reproduced, distributed or transmitted in any form or by any means, including photocopying, recording, or other electronic or mechanical methods, without the prior written permission of the publisher, except in the case of brief quotations embodied in critical reviews and certain other noncommercial uses permitted by copyright law. For permission requests, write to the publisher, addressed "Attention: Permissions Coordinator," at the website below.

www.ZamizPress.com

Quantity sales. Special discounts are available on quantity purchases by corporations, associations, and others. To request pricing, use the author website.

www.MarieWhiteAuthor.com

This Book is For You: How to Find Your Passion & Purpose, From the Mother of an Abducted Child / Marie White —1st ed
ISBN-13: 978-0-9992601-9-7

Cover Design: M.W. Interior Image: Pixabay
Book Layout ©2018 BookDesignTemplates

"Marie makes a connection with your soul, through truth and very raw emotions. It is as if she is reaching out to hold your hand and then saying "Come on, I am walking this journey with you. You are not alone."

-**Heidi Bond**
Author of *Who's the New Kid*

"This is an outstanding book... I highly recommend it and wish it had been around at the beginning of my journey."

-**Dr. Carlos Rivera**
pediatrician and radio
host of *In the Best Interest of the Children*

"Christians who hand their pain to God, will find out that He is big enough."

-**Steve Carter**
founder of Playbook to Millions
international speaker and success coach

"You don't have to hurt as much as you are. Anybody can crawl out of a deep hole. This book is designed to help you see that."

-**Dr. Sue Cornbluth**
host of *The Doctor Sue Show*

"When I saw this, I knew it was exactly what people needed. Marie makes a horrific topic—inspiring!

-**Bill Walsh**
CEO Powerteam International
America's Small Business Expert

Contents

Part One 1
Beginning the Journey 7
   A Peek into our Story 10
There are Three Wars 13
   Emotional 13
   Physical 16
   Spiritual 19
You Can't Trust Your Head 25
Holding on to Hope 29
   What We Do Matters... 34
   Thoughts and Prayer... 38
When Seasons Come 43
   Terrible Milestones 45
   A Sacrifice... 50
The Battle Inside 53
Giving it all Away 59
   Potato Sack Promises 64
Strength from Above 67
   A New Normal 71
The Super Chicken 75
When Your Pain is the Gift 81
   Fear.. 84
   Chosen... 92
They Can't Steal Your Joy 95

Family Problems 101
The Final Curtain 105

Part Two 113
Hearing from Others 115
   The Private Detective 115
   The Reunification Coach 124
   The Grief Doctor 131
   The Sports Therapist 137
   The Trumphant Father 141
Endnotes & Links 149
A Gift for You 151
Hotlines 153
Thanks 155

Part Three 157
Inspiration Cards 161
Daily Checklists 177

To Jason, my rock.

Friendship is born at that moment when one person says to another: What! You too? I thought I was the only one.

—C.S. Lewis

INTRODUCTION

The Backstory

When I sat down to write *Strength for Parents of Missing Children*, I thought I was writing a book for parents like us. Parents who were grieving a living child and trying desperately to survive the wait until their child came home. We learned so much about making it through hard times and there had been no guidebook for us. *Strength* would be a first-of-its-kind survival manual for parents of "missing" children. But the end result turned out to be so much more.

I didn't want to write a book full of my opinions. I wanted to give practical tools to hurting people and share tips from others parents going through similar situations. I was surprised to find that there were dozens of Facebook support groups for parents who had been separated from their children due to divorce. Some of those parents had been awarded custody, yet had been denied access to their children by their ex-spouses. For those parents, legal rights had gone out the window and law enforcement didn't understand parental alienation syndrome (PA or PAS) well enough to enforce the judge's custody orders. Many of those parents were dealing with international abductions of their innocent children by an ex-spouse. They fought for years, as international custody and abduction laws vary from country to country.

I witnessed the daily suicides of parents who couldn't take the pain and fear anymore.

My mission became clearer.

Not only was I writing for parents whose children had been abducted, but also for parents who knew where their children were, but were denied access to them. These parents had to rely on self-control beyond most people's understanding. They had to stop themselves from stealing back their own children. These parents often endured five to ten years of legal battles, costing them hundreds of thousands of dollars.

Once *Strength* was released, I was in for another surprise. Letters, reviews and social media feedback began pouring-in from doctors, therapists, estranged parents and pastors, all wrote about how much the book impacted them. Then foster parents began to recommend it to one another in foster care groups. I read a post about *Strength* that said, "Yes, I've heard nothing but good things about this book."

Really? I thought. *Who* is talking about it?

A contributor from the Huffington Post did an article about the book. Actor Kevin Sorbo of *Hercules* fame, did a video endorsement.

As the book stayed at number one in several Amazon categories and remained in the top three of Amazon's hot new releases for weeks, it became obvious that something special was happening.

Offering people hope was becoming a movement.

Letters and emails came in from people who did not have any connection to missing children, people who read *Strength* out of curiosity and they wrote in to say that reading it had impacted their lives in incredible ways. They felt a renewed purpose in life. They had the desire to do what we had done, to overcome the darkness. They endeavored to discover what they were passionate about and pursue it.

When *Strength* went to Audible for audiobook production, I received an email through my website. The narrator wrote to say that she had stopped recording, in order to send me a message. She had auditioned to narrate my book because she was the parent of two drug-addicted, adult children. When she saw the title and description, she knew she wanted to read the book. During the recording process, she felt compelled to send an email saying that everything I wrote about in the book had applied to her. She has given me permission to share her story.

"This book is for me!" she wrote.

Suddenly, a new group of parents began to read the book, parents of drug-addicted children.

You never know where life is going to take you. Sometimes, you have a clear path that you know you are supposed to take, and at other times the most you can do is put one foot in front of the other. You hope you're on the right track.

As I took each tentative step, doors began to open.

The next thing I knew, I was at the City Gala Grammy after-party, rubbing elbows with John Travolta, Halle Berry, Anthony Mackie (Falcon in Marvel's *Avengers*), Andy Dick, John Paul DeJoria, Russel Simmons, Jeff Timmons (of 98 Degrees), Marcello Thedford and Vern Troyer.

I had to pinch myself, *this* was my life?

Inch by inch, I was thrust into unfamiliar situations.

Forbes top ten influencer, Warren Whitlock, was my guest at an exclusive party at the Foundation Room atop the Mandalay Bay in Las Vegas. Then I was invited to do a TEDx talk. My YouTube channel amassed nearly a million views and dozens of media outlets invited me onto their shows. I attended the launch party for Rock Against Trafficking with actor Rob Morrow and music icon Garry Miller.

If my heart hadn't been so heavy, I would've been living the dream.

In a recent interview I was asked if I would stop writing and speaking when my child came home.

"If it were up to me," I answered, "I'd drop everything and focus 100% on my child. But, I think that God wants me to find a way to keep sharing the message that He is in good even in hard times. And I believe He wants me to share it even after our child comes home. I'm doing what He designed me to do. People's lives are being changed by our story and that's part of my child's legacy. I can't stop. Slow down? Yes. But stop sharing God's goodness with the world? Never."

That's where this book comes in. My time with you, between these pages, is precious. If there was one lesson that I've learned from this whole ordeal it would be that we are precious to God and that He is calling out to you and I. If we don't listen, we just might miss it. My hope is that as you and I share this time together, you will come to realize that God created you for a purpose. You were given gifts that not many others have. It's your destiny to turn over every rock until you find out who God made you to be.

I

Part One

CHAPTER 1

Beginning the Journey

Though I've never met you, I can relate in some way to your struggle. None of us make it through hard times because we are exceptional or strong or smart. We do it because we are forced to. Getting my child back is usually my first thought in the morning, last thought at night, and fills every moment in-between.

What are the spiritual aspects of going through hard times? How can you combat the stress that your body and mind are under? How will your family cope and find purpose during a struggle?

There is beauty in the journey, regardless of the outcome. Let's grieve and hope and fight, together.

There is a hero inside of you. You are the main character in an epic struggle between good and evil. Let's travel to the dark places of grief and climb out, where we can see the bigger picture.

Shakespeare wrote, "Some are born great, some achieve greatness, and some have greatness thrust upon them." That is true of you as well. I will speak to you as though you are going through the same things I have gone through, because there are similarities in our journeys, no matter what the circumstances. You can either be crushed by the hard parts of life and lose your sanity, your family and your life. Or, you can take this pain that was thrust upon you, to propel you into greatness. You can make it through this, even though it's hard.

How does someone keep their faith when their child is abducted? In your own life, how do you make it through the darkest days? Why have bad things happened to you? How could God allow this?

Make up your mind ahead of time to forgive me. I will offend you. Our friends, in their attempts at consolation, have done it to us a thousand times. When words are said that cut your heart into a million pieces, remember that nobody says the right thing all the time.

Trust me with your heart and with your pain. Some things may be hard to hear, but you're becoming an expert at really hard things and you are much stronger than you think.

If you're hurting, I know your pain, when a day without tears is rare and holidays rip you apart. From the falling leaves to the coming of spring, each special moment of the year is dulled by pain.

Looking back on our journey I see the beauty that was in those hard times. From the ashes of my old life a new person has emerged, more caring, more sensitive, stronger and full of deeper purpose. I know that God is still in control, even in the moments when it feels like He has abandoned us, or as H.G. Wells said, "If there is no God, nothing matters. If there is a God, nothing else matters."

***

As a little girl I was terrified of the horrifying screeches cats made at night. Breathing beneath my covers, it seemed like an eternity before I could fall asleep. It wasn't until I dreamt that a cat came after my baby sister that I stopped being afraid. Protecting her filled me with courage and I wrestled the cat to the ground. In that moment, I realized that if I was fighting for someone else, I could be fearless.

And so can you. You are learning to be fearless and becoming who you were always meant to be. You were meant to be a warrior.

It is no coincidence that throughout the Bible God refers to us as soldiers going into battle. Right now we are battling spiritual forces on our knees.

First, realize that we are in a war, an epic battle between good and evil. Right now you feel like evil has won. When something terrible happens, you are never more aware that life is a battlefield.

John Eldridge wrote, "Life is now a battle and a journey. This is the truest explanation of what is going on, the only way to rightly understand our experience ... Life is a desperate quest through dangerous country to a destination that is beyond our wildest hopes, indescribably good."

The destination is indescribably good, not the journey.

You are standing in the middle of a battle. As you watch people being destroyed, remember that war *here* is only preparation for a future which God says is without fear or heartbreak (Revelation 21:4).

But how do you fight this battle and what exactly are you fighting for? Let's find out in the next chapter as we learn to create our battle plan.

Until you know that life is war, you cannot know what prayer is for.
—John Piper

Journal entry, one week into our journey:

I imagine that tomorrow should be the last day of all-day crying. I can feel the tears beginning to taper off. We are in the dark as to what God is going to do. But 2 Thessalonians 3:1-3 says, "As for other matters, brothers and sisters, pray for us that the message of the Lord may spread rapidly and be honored, just as it was with you. And pray that we may be delivered from wicked and evil people, for not everyone has faith. But the Lord is faithful, and he will strengthen you and protect you from the evil one."

I know that it has only been a little over a week, but it feels like our child has been gone forever. How foolish of me to lament what is not even a speck of dust compared to eternity, but I still cry.

I miss my child. I cry out to God all day, "How much longer, Lord?" I know that I will look back and see that only a moment passed and that God used that moment in a mighty way. He has a plan for this time and it's necessary to accomplish His purpose. But it's still painful and I just want it to be over.

However, I trust God's timeline. He will have to make me strong enough to hold on until then. Last night I was praying and shedding tears until a little past midnight. I missed my child so much that I could hardly breathe.

I asked God:
Why?
How long?
How much pain do we have to endure?
What are we supposed to learn from this?
What is Your plan?

Right now, my family depends on me to keep them in a good place. I have to be strong for them. They are all watching me and if I crumble, they crumble too. The old saying is true, "If momma ain't happy, ain't nobody happy."

I go in the garden and put headphones in both ears, blasting the music. If I want to sing along then I am free to do so. There is no one outside at six in the morning.

I usually start out with songs that mimic the cry of my heart.

I cry a lot in the garden.

After a little while I find myself looking up at the sky and praising God for His goodness, bigger than the sky. He is watching over our child, my family and I. He is big enough. He is still good.

A few months after our child was abducted I remember looking in the mirror at church, not recognizing the person I saw. I thought, "How can I look this put together, when I'm falling apart inside?"

Some days were on-the-floor, open-mouth-sobbing, kind of days. I would try to keep it together and finally I would put down the broom, shut my bedroom door and give in to the pain.

Sobbing on the floor, was where I needed to be. Then, when the sobs felt forced, I got up, wiped my face and went back to sweeping.

Three years later I still want to tell everyone I meet at the store or on the street that our child is missing. They need to know. How can the world keep turning while our child is gone?

Through this horrible event I have become aware that every person goes through serious trials. You and I know, in a way that no one else does, that we will never be the same.

But what if we aren't supposed to be? William Arthur Ward wrote, "Adversity causes some men to break: others to break records."

In the coming chapters, we will learn about suffering and hope in this evil world. We will venture into the "valley of the shadow of death" and see if we can make it out alive.

Are you ready? Let's look at the three aspects of our lives that are being attacked right now and how we can combat them.

CHAPTER 2

There are Three Wars

The battle you and I are facing is multi-faceted. During hard times, we face the reality that our emotions are no longer in our control, the reality of what stress is doing to our body and the spiritual reality that a good God seems to have failed us.

Emotional

Our emotional reality is the first battlefront we need to address. If we don't have this under control, then we can't address the other two, because grief holds us down like a weighted blanket.

Like you, I began this journey with days where I had to pry myself out the bed. It took work to get up, be active, and even to eat. Every act felt like trying to walk while dragging a broken leg.

In the beginning you are hanging on by a very thin thread. Your emotions are volatile. Something as simple as a commercial or song can send your body into convulsing sobs. Your world is bleak. It feels like you're wearing dark sunglasses all the time. It is not your imagination that even sunny days seem overcast.

In *Grieving: Our Path Back to Peace*, James R. White wrote, "I have no energy. I feel as if there is a weight lying upon my chest, holding me back, making it difficult to get up in the morning or do anything all day long. I can't concentrate. Tasks that used to be easy for me are now difficult. The future looks so black and bleak. There's just too much to handle. I don't know how I can go on."

The first few weeks my emotions were all over the place and I could hardly eat. I was awake all night with fears playing out in my mind. Having an empty stomach made it even more difficult to eat and after three days of forcing back nausea, I gave myself permission to vomit.

As a former foster parent, having traumatized children in our home had allowed me to see the effect stress and trauma had on the body. I knew there had to be additional measures our family could take to fulfil the obligations of daily life, and continue to hope toward our child's return.

I found things like liquid yogurt, smoothies, soup— anything that could be quickly gulped— alleviated the gag reflex that was caused by stress. After a few days, this liquid diet allowed me to eat again.

Sports performance expert, Dr. Alan Goldberg says that, "Experiencing intense stomach upset, throat constriction or actually throwing up … is a symptom of you being 'in the red zone' as far as your level of physiological arousal goes[2]."

While this is a normal experience for a football player or gymnast, people going through crisis may experience it 24-7 for days, weeks, or even months.

One way to handle the stress is to develop a routine for making it through the day. Here are some practices that are absolutely necessary.

1. <u>Sunlight</u> (at least one hour per day): According to the Mayo Clinic, "Reduced sunlight can cause a drop in serotonin that may trigger depression.[3]" The symptoms of depression; exhaustion, not caring about important things,

feeling overwhelmed and crying, decrease our ability to fight for our child.

2. <u>Go outside</u> (at least 30 minutes per day): The article *The Effects of Sunlight and Fresh Air on the Body*[4] says, "Inhaling fresh air helps clear your lungs and enables you to take deeper, longer breaths of air —which increases the amount of oxygen that's transported to your body's cells. Increased oxygen in your body translates to greater energy and clarity of mind. According to a group of studies published in a 2010 issue of the 'Journal of Environmental Psychology,' research participants reported feeling happier, healthier and more alive when they spent time in nature."

3. <u>Eat a banana.</u> "Bananas are the king of mood-boosting superfoods, offering a rapid enhancement of mood soon after you eat them. The antidepressant effects of bananas most likely come from its dopamine, tryptophan and high vitamin B6 levels.[5]"

4. <u>Only listen, watch or read uplifting things.</u> Author Steve Pavlina writes, "After 30-60 minutes of listening to someone like Zig Ziglar talk about goals, I invariably feel very optimistic and focused. And I tend to get a lot of high-priority work done when I'm in that kind of emotional state. But the key was for me was to maintain this as a daily habit...Whenever I've fallen out of this habit for weeks or months at a time, I've invariably gotten sucked down into negative emotional states. Then I remember my solution, plug back in, and my attitude and productivity shoot back up again[6]."

Visit www.MarieWhiteAuthor.com for a free eBook containing Zig Ziglar videos.

When life is hard you cannot afford to break down, get stuck, or freeze. Keep moving. The best way to do this is to put our bodies on autopilot while our minds are trying to work out solutions to our problems. You do this, as *The Power of Habit* describes, by creating positive habits that allow you to rejuvenate while being under extreme pressure.

Avoid thinking about anything negative.

You have to avoid thinking about anything negative during this time. We will discuss this further in another chapter. For now it's important to concentrate on catching yourself. When you start to go down a negative road, stop the thought. When your mind wanders to the worst case scenario, STOP. When you start thinking of all the wrong that's been done to you, STOP. When you feel yourself contemplating the injustice of it all, STOP.

This is part of your training program. Thinking of these things is harmful to your physical and mental state. There will be a time to think of these, it's just not now.

There will be a time to think on the bad, but not now.

Turn to the Week One Checklist at the end of this book. Check off the boxes daily. The simple act of finishing the list each day will give your body a tiny zap of pleasure and will help you to continue moving forward.

Physical

The second type of reality to address is physical. Is your body under stress? As you go through crisis, your body over-produces stress hormones and eats up any B vitamins in your system. This causes decreased focus, feeling overwhelmed, exhaustion, increased blood pressure and being on-edge all the time.

- Inability to focus
- Feeling overwhelmed

- Exhausted
- High blood pressure
- On-edge

As the Mayo Clinic describes it:

> When you encounter a perceived threat … your hypothalamus, a tiny region at the base of your brain, sets off an alarm system in your body. Through a combination of nerve and hormonal signals, this system prompts your adrenal glands, located atop your kidneys, to release a surge of hormones, including adrenaline and cortisol.
>
> Adrenaline increases your heart rate, elevates your blood pressure and boosts energy supplies. Cortisol, the primary stress hormone, increases sugars (glucose) in the bloodstream…
>
> Vitamin B-12 and other B vitamins play a role in producing brain chemicals that affect mood and other brain functions. Low levels of B-12 and other B vitamins such as vitamin B-6 and folate may be linked to depression[7].

To take care of your physical state, you must work-off some of the adrenaline flooding your system. Otherwise, that pent-up frustration causes the feeling that you are about to pop.

You need exercise. Whether it's walking three miles a day or working out for half an hour, you have to do something. If you don't, the stress will consume you.

Combine the requirements of sunlight, time outside and exercise by walking for an hour a day. This allows your brain and body the downtime that it needs to function properly. Include a friend, and it will also take care of your need for connection and emotional support.

GRIEF

While there are different types of grief, the physical symptoms remain the same. Grieving is usually associated with death and means dealing with an event that has happened, is over, and cannot be fixed. For many people the grief they experience is more like having cancer.

The event is still ongoing, may or may not have an endpoint and has many opportunities for you to help or hinder healing.

For families like ours, how we respond to the trauma is important. If a child has been taken by social services or an ex-spouse, the parents behavior can have a direct effect on the outcome. With runaways and abduction, they fear that if they leave the house, they may miss their child's return.

Each of these scenarios causes trauma and results in Post Traumatic Stress Disorder (PTSD) or Complex Post Traumatic Stress Disorder (C-PTSD).

> Psychologically, the bottom line of trauma is overwhelming emotion and a feeling of utter helplessness.
> —Jon Allen, *Coping with Trauma*

Trauma has been defined as something stressful that is ongoing and unpredictable.

Have you noticed that you involuntarily hold your breath when you check your email, your mail or your phone messages? If so, this is your body's stress reaction.

You may also have noticed that your heart rate increases, you start to sweat and your body is flooded with adrenaline during certain events. These are also stress reactions.

***

In *The 5 Stages of Grief and Other Lies That Don't Help Anyone*[1], the author states that;

> Many people, even professional psychologists, believe there is a right way and a wrong way to grieve, that there is an orderly and predictable pattern that everyone will go through, and if you don't progress correctly, you are failing at grief...
>
> This is a lie.
>
> ...I understand why people—both the griever and those witnessing grief—want some kind of road map, a clearly delineated set of steps or stages that will guarantee a successful end to the pain of grief. The truth is, grief is as individual as love: every life, every path, is unique. There is no predictable pattern, and no linear

progression. Despite what many 'experts' say, there are no stages of grief.

***

The stages of grief she is referring to are:
1. Denial
2. Anger
3. Bargaining
4. Depression
5. Acceptance

If you have experienced a traumatic event you may be grieving. Are you grieving the loss of your family, the loss of your belief that the world is fair, the loss of your trust in God, the loss of people who you thought would stand beside you, or the loss of everything that you once thought unshakable? By themselves those losses would be enough to grieve about, but together they can seem unbearable.

For parents like us, when our children are missing, we don't know who we are or where we fit in this world. Part of our identity has been taken.

The most significant aspect of life is what it does to us spiritually, as we will see in the next section.

You may be grieving:
- The loss of your "normal"
- The loss of belief in a fair world
- The loss of people
- The loss of identity

Spiritual

When life goes wrong the grieving process involves going from one extreme emotion to another. In a period of five minutes you could go from laughter, to anger, to crying. The ground is unstable. One minute you're trusting God and the next you're shaking your fist at

Him. After all, if this could happen, what else could happen? You are bombarded with the fear that you are unprotected.

This overwhelming terror leaves you wondering how a good God could allow this?

Some people decide there can't be a God. Others think that if there is, He doesn't care about them. However, the Bible says that not only is God good, but that we should expect hard times.

- Dear friends, do not be surprised at the fiery ordeal that has come on you to test you, as though something strange were happening to you (1 Peter 4:12).
- Do not be surprised, my brothers and sisters, if the world hates you (1 John 3:13).
- If you see the poor oppressed in a district, and justice and rights denied, do not be surprised at such things (Ecclesiastes 5:8).

The encouragement in these verses is not that bad things happen; it's that what you are going through is *still* under God's control.

Romans 8:28 says, "We know that all things work together for the good of those who love God: those who are called according to His purpose."

There is something different about a Christian going through this type of event. One thing that the Christian has is God's comfort; 2 Corinthians 1:3-4 says, "Praise be to the God and Father of our Lord Jesus Christ, the Father of compassion and the God of all comfort, who comforts us in all our troubles, so that we can comfort those in any trouble with the comfort we ourselves receive from God."

We can rest assured that God holds us in His arms during this ordeal because God says, "I will never leave you nor forsake you," (Hebrews 13:5).

Another thing we have is hope.

Brothers and sisters, we don't want you to be ignorant about those who have died. We don't want you to grieve like other people who have no hope (1 Thessalonians 4:13 GW).

Not only that, but we rejoice in our sufferings, knowing that suffering produces endurance, and endurance produces character, and character produces hope, and hope does not put us to shame (Romans 5:3-5 ESV).

We're not supposed to grieve like those who "have no hope." We grieve with hope and comfort that God sees what is going on and is working behind the scenes.

Maybe God has entrusted you and I with this monumental task for a reason. Can we demonstrate that nothing can make us turn away from God, no matter what He allows? Can we wait to see how God will pull off the miracle of making something good from our hard times?

> Jesus promised his disciples three things—that they would be completely fearless, absurdly happy, and in constant trouble.
> — G.K. Chesterton

In the Bible, Job loses all his children, his possessions, and his health. People watch him deal with the pain of losing everything, and he tells them, "But (God) knows the way that I take; when he has tested me, I will come forth as gold" (Job 23:10).

The word *test* here means to put metal into a hot furnace and separate the gold from other impurities, like lead. Google defines the word *test* as a noun which means "a procedure intended to establish the quality, performance or reliability of something, especially before it is taken into widespread use." If that is what God is doing to you, then He is about to use you in a huge way, and He is establishing your performance.

Job realized this. He knew that for whatever reason, God had allowed these things to happen to him. Job had faith that in the end, God would use them to make Job pure, like precious gold. You and I have been given the task of living through hard things, but in the end we can become part of something monumental.

WAITING

You don't have to do this alone. God gives you promises to cling to while you wait. His first promise to Christians is that He will work everything out for a good purpose both now and for eternity.

"We know that all things work together for the good of those who love God: those who are called according to His purpose (Romans 8:28 HCSB)."

The second promise is that He will personally comfort you while you go through this.

> Shout for joy, you heavens; rejoice, you earth; burst into song, you mountains! For the Lord comforts his people and will have compassion on his afflicted ones (Isaiah 49:13).

Even with God's comfort, the battle is not over. We still have an enemy out there who wants to destroy our joy, our hope, our families and our destiny. You have to fight against Satan's whisper of, "Did God really say?" (Genesis 3:1) to every promise that God gives.

You know the whispers:
- "Did God really say that all things work together for the good of those who love Him, if He allowed this?"
- "How will God comfort you? He can't appear and hold you."
- "Are you sure that God says to hope? You don't deserve good things."

No matter what you feel like today, you are here for a purpose. Right now your purpose is to participate in an event where the outcome will show just how good God is.

He is good. No matter what we feel like today.

- Surely God is good to Israel, to those who are pure in heart (Psalm 73:1).
- For the Lord God is a sun and shield; the Lord bestows favor and honor; no good thing does he withhold from those whose walk is blameless (Psalm 84:11).

- You keep track of all my sorrows. You have collected all my tears in your bottle. You have recorded each one in your book (Psalm 56:8 NLT).

TEARS

God keeps our tears in a bottle. That means that He sees every drop and those tears are not wasted. He isn't collecting them for no reason. He is using our tears to produce something.

> *Those who sow with tears*
> *will reap with songs of joy.*
> *Those who go out weeping,*
> *carrying seed to sow,*
> *will return with songs of joy,*
> *carrying sheaves with them.*
> *—Psalm 126:5-6*

Since ancient times no one has heard, no ear has perceived, no eye has seen any God besides you, who acts on behalf of those who wait for him (Isaiah 64:4).

The devil wants to make you believe that God's promises aren't true. When it feels like the devil is whispering lies to your heart, remember that God says He will never leave you or forsake you, (Deuteronomy 31:6) and there must be a bigger plan.

King David wrote:

> *I would have despaired*
> *unless I had believed*
> *that I would see the goodness of the Lord*
> *In the land of the living.*
> *Wait for the Lord;*
> *Be strong and let your heart take courage;*
> *Yes, wait for the Lord.*
> *—Psalm 27:13-14 NASB*

On the days when you're being hit again and again, remember to take courage and wait for God.

Greg Laurie has two talks about suffering that I want to share at www.MarieWhiteAuthor.com. Go to the "Strength for Parents" tab and click Book Links 1 and 2.

Listen to those two talks before moving on to the next chapter, because we are going to build on the theme. Something amazing is about to happen.

Steps to remember:
- Create a new routine
- Stop thinking about negative things
- Use the weekly checklist

CHAPTER 3

You Can't Trust Your Head

As I write this, our child has been gone for over three years. I know what it's like to wait with bated breath. I also know what it's like to have moments of despair.

In the beginning of a hard journey, your days are full of every emotion. If you wake up sad, by breakfast you can go from sadness to anger. By lunch, you may move from frustration to numbness. The most you can manage is survival.

Greg Laurie talks a lot about the effect his son's death had on his life. He said that it was the worst thing that could ever happen to a parent, but I would disagree, even death seems preferable to the horrors I've been left to imagine.

But that's the problem; I'm not supposed to imagine those things. 2 Corinthians 10:3-5 NET says:

> For though we live as human beings, we do not wage war according to human standards, for the weapons of our warfare are not human weapons, but are made powerful by God for tearing down strongholds. We tear down arguments and every arrogant obstacle that is raised up against the knowledge of God, and we take every thought captive to make it obey Christ.

Look where it says to "take every thought captive."

I have felt disobedient every time I thought about what my child *might* be enduring.

Not the sick-to-your-stomach feeling of fear, but the feeling of guilt. It's been God's way of convicting me to "take every thought captive."

I could tell myself that thinking about these things doesn't change anything. It only makes me scared, sad and angry. It speeds up my heart rate, increases my blood pressure, and floods my system with the stress hormones—cortisol and adrenaline. But everything in me still *wants* to think about what's happening to my child.

Whatever is true, whatever is noble, whatever is right, whatever is pure, whatever is lovely, whatever is admirable—if anything is excellent or praiseworthy—think about such things (Philippians 4:8).

Training our minds to think only on the true, noble, right, pure, lovely, admirable, excellent and praiseworthy is not easy. But it is part of our training program, it's like Crossfit® for spiritual warfare.

In the midst of all that has happened, we are supposed to grow physically and spiritually. We are supposed to get stronger.

That means that you must control the things you think about and listen to. You're not allowing your mind time to think about evil.

Corrie Ten Boom said, "Worry does not empty tomorrow of its sorrow, it empties today of its strength."

The idea of taking every thought captive is harder than it sounds. For the first year, I had to listen to podcasts in the shower. Why? Because in the shower I had just enough time to be filled with doubt and fear. It's a matter of forcing yourself to focus on the good and not give in to worry.

Until the day we see God's good purpose, He is asking us to trust Him in the dark.

Focus your thoughts to remember all of the times that God has been faithful to you. James MacDonald says:

To heighten the miraculous, God makes us wait—but also to prepare the recipient. Waiting is the process by which God makes us spiritually fit to receive what He has *all along* determined to do.

Let me just ask you this about your trial, do you want to win or do you want to win big? The signs of God's presence should be obvious. Scan the landscape of your life. Can you not produce some signs that God is working? He doesn't just want to win. He wants to win in a way that you know it's Him. He led you into the trial. He's going to lead you out.

If God allowed these hard times, then there must be a reason. Your mission is to use this time for all it's worth, to accomplish any task that *might* be the reason God allowed it.

We must be strong and wait.

In the next chapter we will look at hopelessness and how to combat it.

Steps to remember:
- Take your thoughts captive
- Have music, audiobooks, or sermons playing in one ear
- Don't allow your mind to drift back to negative things

And we know that in all things God works for the good of those who love him, who have been called according to his purpose (Romans 8:28).

Enjoy this article by Michael Ramsden called, *How Can I Believe in God and Pain* at www.MarieWhiteAuthor.com. Go to the "Strength for Parents" tab and click Book Link 3.

CHAPTER 4

Holding on to Hope

How did we make it through those first tough weeks? I think Tom Hanks in *Sleepless in Seattle* said it best, "I'm going to get out of bed every morning. Breathe in and out all day long. And then after a while, I won't have to remind myself to get out of bed every morning and breathe in and out."

If you're suffocating in your hard time, let me assure you that it does get better and you won't have to make yourself get out of bed every morning.

> Faith does not eliminate questions.
> But faith knows where to take them.
> —Elisabeth Elliot

For several months, I would get up, get dressed, eat, and mechanically complete the tasks of the day. Meanwhile, everything within me was screaming in anguish. All I really wanted to do was hide under the covers and wake up when this was all over. But life doesn't work that way. Even if I could have stayed in bed all day, what would that have accomplished? It would only make me feel worse, because I had wasted a day.

The last thing that you need is to feel more pain.

Some days I have to pray the moment I wake up, "Lord, tell me *again* that it's going to be okay. Hold me in Your arms, like a little child, and remind me that everything will be all right." Then during the day, I hear a song and take a deep breath, and my shoulders relax. Only then do I realize that my shoulders were up and I hadn't taken any deep breaths.

There will be days when your physical pain or mental anguish aren't the first things on your mind in the morning and the last things on your mind at night. You will survive. You can make it, as many people have before you.

In our case we had to realize that abduction was not a new event. Whatever you are going through, the Bible has an example of someone going through something similar.

There were many people in the Bible who were abducted and sold into slavery, or taken captive. Even in their captivity, these people had powerful lives for God. Some abductions, like those mentioned in Isaiah 39:5-7, were even foretold decades in advance.

Four very famous abductees were, Daniel, Shadrach, Meshach and Abednego. These teenagers were ripped from their families, and taken to another country, to serve the enemy king. They were put through a rigorous training program to rid them of their old identities. Instead these boys became a light to others in the darkness. They stood for God, and helped rule the country.

Joseph was kidnapped by his brothers and sold into slavery, only to become the second in command over all of Egypt.

A young girl was kidnapped to be a servant for the enemy commander. Instead of being bitter, she cared for her master and sent him to the prophet Elisha, where he was cured of leprosy.

They each had a choice to make. It's the same one you and I face, either we can emerge from this event warped, or we can come through it changed into something new. At the conclusion of *Lord of the Rings*, Frodo had become so warped by carrying the one ring and traveling the hard journey, that he could not return to normal life. But his companion also carried the ring, took the same journey. Going through the journey taught Sam that life was short and he used this new perspective to boldly pursue life.

At the beginning of the journey Frodo started strong and his companion was weak. Frodo ends the journey broken. His companion finishes the journey strengthened.

This illustrates the beauty of God's transforming power through adversity. He can use adversity to make the weak strong and the strong weak.

The song *Save My Life* by Sidewalk Prophets, talks about crying out to God, asking Him to remind us that we are not alone. It begs God to tell us again that He has not forgotten us. Sometimes we feel completely alone and we need Him to tell us that there is still hope, even when we're suffocating in despair.

> Sometimes we feel completely alone.

We need to remember there are details we can't see.

If our life was a movie, how many times did we have a near miss where God intervened on our behalf? And did we give Him credit? No, because we never knew.

Priscilla Shirer says it like this, "He can see more than we can see, and He can love us without needing to explain why His love needs to look like this at the moment."

But is there still hope? Can God make some sort of good out of the hard parts of your life? Do we have any concrete examples of God working behind the scenes?

> She could hide him no longer. The baby whom she had nursed and protected and kept hidden for three precious yet-sleepless months was gone. Whatever was to become of him in his makeshift cradle-boat, she knew she would never lay eyes on him again. And in that room—in all of Egypt, in the hearts of many, God was at work. There she sat. A woman who feared The Lord, who waited on Him expectantly, but who had seen with her own eyes that for her

people, waiting meant slavery, toil, injustice, and death. And then she saw her—through the window, down the alley, her daughter Miriam running, breathless, calling to her mother. God had indeed been at work![8]

In that paragraph we are allowed to trade places with Moses' mother, and imagine how alone and abandoned she must have felt, only to find that God had been working things out all along.

Before Shadrach, Meshach and Abednego, how many people in fiery furnaces were killed?

All of them.

Before Daniel, how many people thrown into the lion's den were ripped to shreds?

All of them.

In Egypt, before Moses was born, how many Israelite baby boys were either born into slavery or killed?

All of them!

Do you see a pattern?

God is architect of the miraculous. Just because something doesn't normally happen, does not mean that God is going to let it continue that way. It only takes once for a new pattern to emerge.

The Bible says that God will punish those who hate Him, "but showing love to a thousand generations of those who love me and keep my commandments" (Exodus 20:6).

We know that God is able.

The question then becomes, "Is God willing?"

He is, my friend.

When young David stood before the giant, Goliath, David yelled:

> You come against me with sword and spear and javelin, but I come against you in the name of the Lord Almighty (1 Samuel 17:45).

Before we move on to our role in all of this, I would like you to watch these two videos, to see how God uses pain at www.MarieWhiteAuthor.com. Go to the "Strength for Parents" tab and click Book Links 4 and 5.

>And in despair I bowed my head;
> "There is no peace on earth," I said;
> "For hate is strong
> and mocks the song
> Of peace on earth, good-will to men!"
> Then pealed the bells more loud and deep:
> "God is not dead, nor doth he sleep!
> The Wrong shall fail,
> The Right prevail,
> With peace on earth, good-will to men!"

-Henry Wadsworth Longfellow

What We Do Matters

Some things stay with you forever. Years ago I read an article about a couple who fasted at lunch every Thursday to pray for their children. I thought this was a great idea, but never imagined that I could do it. In the middle of our child being gone, I found that fasting no longer sounded so impossibly hard. I chose Wednesday at lunch and committed to fasting and praying for my family each Wednesday for the rest of my life.

When the disciples had a demon they could not cast out, Jesus said it was because the disciples hadn't fasted and prayed. Since they had not fasted, their prayers were not powerful enough, so Jesus had to cast the demon out for them.

Prayer alone had not broken the evil strongholds that kept our child from coming home. I needed to do something powerful. I decided to start fasting during lunch once a week. Praying and fasting for our missing child, as well as each member of our family, was both the least, and the most, I could do. Fasting is another tool that you can use to fight.

Ravi Zacharias tells the story of a young soldier who was in battle. This man worked as a medic. One day his commanding officer told him to run onto the battlefield and pull the wounded men to safety. The battle was thick. There were bullets flying, and the young man kept looking down at his watch. Then, he would look at the battlefield and hesitate. Over and over he looked out, and then again at his watch. His commander yelled again for him to get out onto the field! Finally, the young man looked at his watch once more, and ran to pull others to safety.

Later his commander confronted him. Why did he take so long to obey the command? The young man stated that though he was not a Christian, his mother was. Before he left she had told him that every day, at that particular time, she would be praying for him. He decided that he was not going to go into battle until he knew that she was praying.

What we do matters.

The simple prayers of a person's heart can have a profound effect on many lives.

If you have children, can you imagine sending them into the world with the knowledge that each week you were fasting and praying for them? That would be a lasting legacy. It would connect you across the miles.

Imagine it, just you and God, talking about the kids.

Would you like to join me on Wednesdays?

Do our prayers *really* achieve anything? Do they actually affect the outcome? The Bible says that they do.

"The prayer from the heart of a man right with God has much power" (James 5:16 NLV).

The verses below, tell of a time when God was looking for someone who would:

...stand in the gap before (Him) so that (He) might not destroy (the city), but (He) found no one. So (He) poured out judgement. God was willing to forgive, but in an entire city there was **not even one** person who would pray for that city. Because there was no one who would pray, the city was destroyed.

> The people of the land have practiced extortion and committed robbery. They have oppressed the poor and needy and unlawfully exploited the foreign resident. I searched for a man among them who would repair the wall and stand in the gap before Me on behalf of the land so that I might not destroy it, but I found no one. So I have poured out My indignation on them and consumed them with the fire of My fury. I have brought their actions down on their own heads (Ezekiel 22:29-31 HCSB).

In Matthew 7:7-8 HCSB, Jesus says that we are supposed to "Keep asking, and it will be given to you. Keep searching, and you will find. Keep knocking, and the door will be opened to you. For everyone who asks receives, and the one who searches finds, and to the one who knocks, the door will be opened."

Look online or in your Bible and find the rest of that paragraph, through verse 12. Verses 9-12 explain how God feels about us asking Him for things.

> C.S. Lewis said:
>
> In every action, just as in every prayer, you are trying to bring about a certain result; and this result must be good or bad. Why, then, do we not argue as the opponents of prayer argue, and say that if the intended result is good God will bring it to pass without your interference, and that if it is bad He will prevent it happening whatever you do? Why wash your hands? If God intends them to be clean, they'll be clean without your washing them...Why do anything? We know that we can act and that our actions produce results ... You cannot be sure of a good harvest whatever you do to a field. But you can be sure that if you pull one weed that one weed will no longer be there ... Prayers are not always— in the crude, factual sense of the word— "granted". This is not because prayer is a weaker kind of causality, but because it is a stronger kind. When it "works" at all it works unlimited by space and time. That is why God has retained discretionary power of granting or refusing it.

We do not always see the immediate results of our prayers. However, we should know that they are doing something in a realm far beyond our ability to comprehend, and are more powerful than we know.

In James MacDonald's book, *When Life is Hard*, he writes about suffering through his son's horrible accident, his church caving in, and getting cancer, all at once.

> Millions of dollars in liens were placed on the stalled project, and dark clouds of bankruptcy loomed large over the entire ministry. Construction committee members resigned *en masse*. Night after night I walked alone through the incomplete worship facility. It felt more like a tomb than a church. And as I walked I wondered how it had all come to this and what God's possible purpose could be in making life so hard.

In the midst of all that James went through, he wrote several books, and produced incredible resources for others who experience hard times.

> The richest testimonies come from people He has made whole
> and who still remember what it was like to be broken.
> —Beth Moore

One of the rewards of going through something hard is that it earns you the right to speak about God's goodness. For someone to hear that God is good, even when they see you suffering, speaks volumes. If you can still trust God when it looks like He has abandoned you, then you must know something about God that they don't. And we do. We know that God has used a thousand hard times and terrible people to bring about His good plans. In fact, it is during hard times that people often feel closest to God.

One of the most famous Christian books of all time is *Pilgrim's Progress*, written in 1678 by John Bunyan. It was written while Bunyan was in prison. The reason he was in jail was that he was a Baptist preacher at a time when the Church of England was the only church allowed.

Bunyan's wife died, his daughter was blind, and he was in prison. You would think that with all of the bad things that had happened to him, he would have been bitter with God. Instead he wrote the most beautiful story about a man who has to go through life's trials to get to heaven. Bunyan takes each season of our lives, and gives it a name and a place. As you read it, your soul begins to heal, and you realize that all of us have to walk through troubles. His book is still a best-seller, which almost every Christian has read, and found comfort in.

Thoughts and Prayer

> The paradox of grief is that it is healing; it somehow restores our souls, when all the while we thought it would leave us in despair.
> —John Eldridge

> We do not want you to be uninformed, brothers and sisters, about the troubles we experienced in the province of Asia. We were under great pressure, far beyond our ability to endure, so that we despaired of life itself. Indeed, we felt we had received the sentence of death. But this happened that we might not rely on ourselves but on God, who raises the dead. He has delivered us from such a deadly peril, and he will deliver us again. On him we have set our hope that he will continue to deliver us (2 Corinthians 1:8-10).

> Do not be anxious about anything, but in every situation, by prayer and petition, with thanksgiving, present your requests to God (Philippians 4:6).

> We also glory in our sufferings, because we know that suffering produces perseverance; perseverance, character; and character, hope. And hope does not put us to shame, because God's love has been poured out into our hearts through the Holy Spirit, who has been given to us (Romans 5:3-5).

Joy and pain together baffle me.

How can we have joy during this heart wrenching time? But some of us do have it. We can also say "thank you" to God because we know Him. It would be similar to being a prisoner of war undergoing brainwashing as the captors say, "You have no country. No one cares about you. You do not have anyone who wants you to return." And how would the prisoner combat the barrage of statements meant to make them forget their homeland? They would combat it by recalling memories of riding a bike through the countryside, drinking a soda with friends, going to prom. They would combat the lies with memories of the truth.

It is the same with God. When you look around and can only see pain and sadness, search your memories, and remember when He has proven Himself faithful to you.

> *Faith thanks God in the middle of the story.*
> —Ann Voskamp

God is always up to something.

I have asked Him what I'm supposed to do. I feel like His answer is, "Go through this."

To which my heart screams, "It's too hard!"

> For the eyes of the LORD run to and fro throughout the whole earth, to show Himself strong on behalf of those whose heart is loyal to Him (2 Chronicles 16:9).

God wants to show Himself strong, and He is happy to do so through people who are willing to let Him have His way.

> When you are brought before synagogues, rulers and authorities, do not worry about how you will defend yourselves or what you will say, for the Holy Spirit will teach you at that time what you should say (Luke 12:11-12).

Everything in the Bible says not to worry or fear. It also says that if you are a Christian, this is His battle, and He already has the victory planned. We are to "be still."

It is still unbelievably hard. While we are looking at our empty arms, it is easy to forget the good things in our lives. We may start to wonder if there are any good things.

Write down anything for which you are thankful. If you need help, start with the most basic things and continue on until you can't write any more. Use paper to finish the list.

Mine would start with:

1. A home to live in
2. Food to eat
3. The privilege to be a parent, when others never get that opportunity, even for a short time
4. A family who loves me
5. Friends
6. Money to pay the bills

7. Hope

Start your list here:

1.

2.

3.

4.

5.

6.

7.

8.

9.

10.

When you thank God and praise Him in the middle of your hardship, you are actually presenting an offering to God. Your thank-offering is worth more to Him than time or money. One of the most precious gifts you can give to God is a thankful heart and trust in Him, especially when you don't understand what He is doing.

Listen to this talk by Greg Laurie, as he walks you through this process. He says that going through hardship earns you the right to speak.

Hear it at www.MarieWhiteAuthor.com. Go to the "Strength for Parents" tab and click Book Link 6.

Steps to remember:
- You will make it
- Abduction isn't new
- Miracles happen
- God is still at work

And we know that in all things God works for the good of those who love him, who have been called according to his purpose (Romans 8:28).

CHAPTER 5

When Seasons Come

Why does time keep marching on?
Every holiday, special event or season, I think, "Our child should be home. God wouldn't want them to miss summer, Easter or Christmas with their family?" Yet the days go by. I dust their bedroom. I vacuum the floor. I plant flowers in the spring, so when they come home the house will look festive. It's the same reason I decorate at Thanksgiving and Christmas. Our child's presents sit wrapped and ready, gathering dust.

When I was at my lowest, I screamed at the ceiling, "How God? How could you allow our child to have a life that was great, and safe, and loving, only to let them be ripped away? How could You do this?"

Some days all I wanted was to be alone in a field, on my knees, hands raised to the sky, screaming, "Come on Lord! Part the sea already! I'm tired. I'm hurting. I'm worn out! How much longer?"

Those were tough days.

I can't wait until this whole mess is over, so that I can fall asleep without a care in the world, like the end of the movie *Groundhog Day*.

We all seem to be faced with the same problems over and over. Forgive those who don't deserve it. Hope through the pain. Trust God. Forgive those who don't deserve it. Hope through the pain. Trust God. Forgive those who don't deserve it. Hope through the pain. Trust God. Don't become bitter.

There are some days that I have to remember we are not supposed to live in fear. Sometimes I forget that.

Fear is my constant enemy. Is it yours?

"What if?" plays at the edge of my mind, waiting to be invited in.

What if our child is being hurt?

What if they don't come home?

What if they have forgotten us?

What if it happens again?

And it goes on.

Then one day, when I was crying out to Him, God did the miraculous.

He answered my, "What ifs."

God was listening.

There will be an end to all of this. How it comes to an end, and why we had to go through this only God knows. Our job is to represent Him in all that we do.

Like Moses said to the Israelites, "Do not be afraid. Stand firm and you will see the deliverance the Lord will bring you today. The Egyptians you see today you will never see again. The Lord will fight for you; you need only to be still" (Exodus 14:13).

Terrible Milestones

Every day, week or month is a terrible milestone. With each passage of time clothes are outgrown, seasons are missed, and we feel like it's been too long.

Every season is painful because we go through it without your child.

It used to be that certain things would remind me of our child, a toy, a sound, a smell. Eventually, everything reminded me of them.

At Thanksgiving we invited several families over to dinner. With our extended family we ate, laughed and prayed together. I could not have imagined any holiday that was not a stabbing reminder that our child was not with us. Looking forward to having people over gave us something to anticipate.

God was with us that day. Wondrously, we had comfort instead of devastation.

So many people came up to us at church and said they were praying for us during the holidays. Their comments only confirmed the feeling I had that, at different moments in the day, someone was praying. Obviously, it was not our normal Christmas. We could not get into the usual rhythm. Our child's stocking hung empty.

I had to catch myself before I could get lost in a memory, or start thinking of what our child was doing at that exact moment. I had to hand my worries to God to let Him take them, and He did.

We had a sense of peace on Christmas Day. We were not sobbing, worried about our child. Periodically each of our eyes filled with tears, and laughter was forced, but God gave us a gift that Christmas. His gift to us was peace for that moment.

In the midst of all this, some people have told us to give up. They weren't trying to be cruel; they were trying to release us from the pain of hoping. I could tell that it was breaking their heart to see us hurting. But it was still hard for us to hear. Snapping at anyone who ever made an insensitive remark would only make them afraid to say anything, and eventually it would make us strangers.

I don't want to go through this alone.

Someone once told us that when comparing our situation to dying refugee children in Syria, ours wasn't that bad. I thought of *Men in Black* when one character is told that it is better to have loved and lost, then to have never loved at all, and the character snaps back, "Try it!" (Watch it at www.MarieWhiteAuthor.com. Click on the "Strength for Parents" tab.)

I also have to avoid the tendency to become overly critical of others. Instead you and I need to see their hearts. *Anything* that someone said to me during the first few weeks hit me wrong. Even when someone said that everything would be fine, I wanted to scream, "How do you know?"

On cold days, I wonder if my child is cold. When the news says that a child has been hurt or a house has caught fire, I watch to see if our child's picture flashes across the screen. But it doesn't, and the world keeps spinning.

What time are they in bed? What time do they wake up? Does anyone pay attention to their needs?

When I start to think about these things I remember that I need to leave those questions in God's hands and let them go. I have to trust Him.

I know that time doesn't stop for anyone. I wish it would though. I would stop time until our child comes home, and then time could start again.

How do I answer the question of how many children we have? How do I answer when someone asks us where our missing child is? Those questions hurt every single time.

I still have days when this is all too much to handle; when everything that I know about God and His plan, doesn't matter. The pain is too much. I can't wrap my head around a reason. But those days come less and less often, and having lived through them before, I know that they will pass. Now, I wait to see how many days they will last. Sometimes it's only one day, and sometimes four or five. Those long spells are the hardest. I'm never sure what sets me off, is it the memory, or the heartache?

Sometimes I shove the pain away until it's over, and sometimes I give in to it. The only difference is that in one case I'm numb, and in the other I cry. Then, one day I wake up and it's gone. Another test passed, another crisis averted. And I'm stronger for the next one, because now I know that it will not last forever.

There are times when all I've done was binge watch TV just to get through the hours without thinking of my child. Sometimes I grab a movie with a happy ending just to remind myself that there are happy endings.

Incidentally, my house is neat as a pin. I keep thinking that if I can just get life organized, then God will bring our child home. I know that I am only fooling myself.

For years I've looked in vain for an article I believe was in *Focus on the Family* magazine. It was about a couple whose son had died. It was unexpected, so it may have been a car accident, but the article was about them putting their special-needs daughter onto the school bus. The bus driver asked them how they were coping, and they said the most unexpected thing. They said that if their son had not died, then they never would have adopted their daughter, and not knowing her would have been an even bigger tragedy.

I didn't understand that.

But, I think that I might understand it now.

God can still give joy in the midst of pain.

It would have been impossible for someone to walk up to this family when they lost their son and tell them that losing their son would lead to another love, another purpose. That would have been heartless to say at their son's funeral. Yet that is exactly what God said to them, and showed them. It's almost as if they discovered how to, "Be joyful in hope, patient in affliction, faithful in prayer" (Romans 12:12).

I never want anyone to be alone in their suffering. For that reason, I've called people I didn't know to tell them that I can relate to what they are going through.

I'm willing to risk their rejection on the chance that someone who is hurting as much as I have been, might find comfort in talking with a fellow parent of a missing child.

Paul says it like this, "Praise be to the God and Father of our Lord Jesus Christ, the Father of compassion and the God of all comfort, who comforts us in all our troubles, so that we can comfort those in any trouble with the comfort we ourselves receive from God. For just as we share abundantly in the sufferings of Christ, so also our comfort abounds through Christ" (2 Corinthians 1:3-5).

> By faith we can choose the future over the moment.
> —James MacDonald

In The Prayer of Jabez, Bruce Wilkinson is explaining to his mentor that he feels scared, confused and out of his element. His mentor says, "that feeling you are running from is called dependence. It means that you are walking with the Lord Jesus. Actually, the second you're not feeling dependent is the second you've backed away from truly living by faith."

Bruce questions him, "that feeling that I just can't do it is what I'm *supposed* to be feeling?" His mentor continues, "As God's chosen, blessed sons and daughters, we are expected to attempt something large enough that failure is guaranteed ... unless God steps in."

The Bible says, "faith is the substance of things hoped for. The substance of things not seen" (Hebrews 11:1).

Like Indiana Jones, we are supposed to take a leap of faith from the lion's mouth. But, just like the movie, we are going to find out that no leap is necessary. What looks like an impossible situation is no problem for God. He is always there to keep us from falling into the abyss.

Each of our battles is different, but as Christians, we are on the winning side between good and evil. We are meant to be warriors.

During this trial of my faith, there have been several tests to my integrity. Times when I had a choice to make: either trust God, or take things into my own hands.

You and I must hold on to our integrity, even in the face of evil.

It takes everything in me to get back up after one of the enemy's sucker-punches. Someone who is fighting on your child's behalf will sometimes kick you from behind, adding insult to injury. You may ask, "Lord, when are you going to stand up for us?"

Remember that this life is only boot camp for eternity. We are called to love and care about this world, while keeping our eyes focused on heaven. I don't know how we can do that without discounting this life we are in. Where is the balance? How do we care about this life and the people in it without losing our focus on eternity?

> My knowledge of this life is small,
> The eye of faith is dim;
> But 'tis enough that Christ knows all,
> And I shall be with Him.
> —Richard Baxter

A Sacrifice

God illustrated His desire to have all of our heart when He asked Abraham to sacrifice his son. He could have asked Abraham for any number of other things. God could have told Abraham to sacrifice all of his livestock. That would have made Abraham destitute. But God did not ask that.

God chose the son of Abraham's favorite wife, the very son that God had promised, and asked Abraham to sacrifice what was most precious to him.

The same with Joseph, Abraham's great-grandson. Jacob had twelve sons, and his favorite was Joseph. Through a twisted series of events, God took Joseph from Jacob.

God also did this with Job. A devoted father, Job took his time teaching his children, training them, loving them and sacrificing for them. When Satan attacked Job, he took Job's livestock and his servants, but nothing hit Job like the death of his children.

Finally, God did it to himself, with His own son.

It is almost as if God is saying, "I want you to be willing to care, to sacrifice and to love the people of this world in abundance. And I want you to be willing to give them all up at the snap of a finger."

A sacrifice is only a sacrifice if it costs us something. God wants us to care. When we care, we invest. When we invest, we are connected. When we are connected, it hurts to let go. When God says to let go, we have to trust Him. When we trust Him, we are intimately connected to Him.

Jesus said, "I am the vine; you are the branches. If you remain in me and I in you, you will bear much fruit; apart from me you can do nothing" (John 15:5).

I still have days when I doubt that God has everything under control and I question His motives. There is ample evidence around me that God is good, but I still wonder about it.

You and I forget that God listens to our hearts, and answers even our unspoken prayers.

Have you lost your faith? Has your ordeal overwhelmed you? Is there any evidence of God working in your life? Are there any good things in your life that indicate that God is with you and for you?

"The Lord said to Moses, "How long will these people despise Me? How long will they not trust in Me despite all the signs I have performed among them?" (Numbers 14:11 HCSB)

> God never withholds from His child that which His love and wisdom call good. God's refusals are always merciful — "severe mercies" at times but mercies all the same. God never denies us our hearts desire except to give us something better. —Elisabeth Elliot

There is an attitude that makes all our troubles fade into the background. It is powerful and virtuous and available anytime. Let's see how to harness that power in the next chapter.

Our troubles seem like more than we can handle—until we see what others have been through and overcome.

Here is the story of a mother who gave to another person, in her grief, and the ripples that touched so many lives. Watch it at www.MarieWhiteAuthor.com. Go to the "Strength for Parents" tab and click Book Link 7.

> And we know that in all things God works for the good of those who love him, who have been called according to his purpose (Romans 8:28).

CHAPTER 6

The Battle Inside

"Sometimes you win and sometimes you _____."

Did you put the word "lose" in the blank? Instead, write the word "learn."

Parents like me have already thought of everything we would have done differently if we had known the last time we had our child, would be the last time we had our child. We can't turn back the hands of time, and if we learn from them, hard experiences don't have to be mistakes.

In the movie, *The Secret Life of Walter Mitty*, Walter will lose his job if he can't find an important man. His life has been plain and ordinary. He longs for more, but the pressures of life have made him feel like boring was all that he could accomplish. When he has to find this man, for the first time in his life he does what *he has always wanted* to do. Walter goes on an epic journey and discovers the man he was meant to be.

It takes a crisis for him to change his life.

This is your crisis.

> People change when they hurt enough that they have to, learn enough that they want to, and receive enough that they are able to.
> —John Maxwell

If your life was a movie, this would be the defining moment. This is the part when the audience would wonder, will this tragedy crush you, or does it push you toward greater things? Do you want this trial to end with you in the fetal position on the floor? Or do you want to be stronger, better, and more in-control than you've ever been?

It is time to reevaluate your life.

Hard times are a turning point in your story. To move on, you need to address anything that is holding you back. Besides fear, there is something else that is stopping you.

There days when you feel like you deserve this.

Have you really done something so terrible that God had to hurt you?

I am going to assume that you have not done anything to make you deserving of this punishment. That means Satan is lying to you when he whispers, "You deserve this. It's all your fault." Or maybe you're lying to yourself. Bad things happen to good people too.

In case you are stuck on the idea that you might deserve this punishment, let's investigate one example of cause and effect, and see if it meets your expectations for God's justice.

It would be worth your time to read the whole story of King David's life, in 2 Samuel chapters 11 and 12. That part of the Bible really helps you understand the training program that God has for each of us.

David was a godly man, whom God used to do incredible acts. But for a moment, we are going to look at when David did some terrible things.

2 Samuel chapter 11 begins, "In the spring, at the time when kings go off to war, David sent Joab out with the king's men…But David remained in Jerusalem."

What was David's royal position?
Where was David?
So, at the time that kings go to war, King David was not going to war. That's problem number one.

One evening David got up from his bed and walked around on the roof of the palace. From the roof he saw a woman bathing. The woman was very beautiful, and David sent someone to find out about her. The man said, 'She is Bathsheba, the daughter of Eliam and the wife of Uriah the Hittite.' Then David sent messengers to get her. She came to him, and he slept with her (2 Samuel 11:2-4).

What did he see while lazing around on the rooftop?
What did he do about it?
So, while King David was skirting his duties as king he saw a naked, married, woman and instead of turning away—he slept with her.

"The woman conceived and sent word to David, saying, 'I am pregnant.'"

How many wrong moves did King David make?

Do you think that those actions were bad enough for God to punish David?

He didn't go to work, had an affair and a child resulted from it. David's transgressions don't end there. He then sends a message to one of his soldiers, Joab. He tells Joab to have the woman's husband killed.

"In the morning David wrote a letter to Joab and sent it with Uriah. In it he wrote, 'Put Uriah out in front where the fighting is fiercest. Then withdraw from him so he will be struck down and die.'"

Does that sound like the behavior of a godly man?

"When Uriah's wife heard that her husband was dead, she mourned for him. After the time of mourning was over, David had her brought to his house, and she became his wife and bore him a son. But the thing David had done displeased the Lord."

Now if you and I were on the jury of a murder trial where a man did not do his job, had an affair, a child was conceived and then the man had the husband murdered, I can only assume that we would ask the judge for a harsh sentence.

> The Lord sent Nathan to David. When he came to him, he said, "There were two men in a certain town, one rich and the other poor. The rich man had a very large number of sheep and cattle, but the poor man had nothing except one little ewe lamb he had bought. He raised it, and it grew up with him and his children. It shared his food, drank from his cup and even slept in his arms. It was like a daughter to him.
>
> Now a traveler came to the rich man, but the rich man refrained from taking one of his own sheep or cattle to prepare a meal for the traveler who had come to him. Instead, he took the ewe lamb that belonged to the poor man and prepared it for the one who had come to him."
>
> David burned with anger against the man and said to Nathan, "As surely as the Lord lives, the man who did this must die! He must pay for that lamb four times over, because he did such a thing and had no pity."
>
> Then Nathan said to David, "You are the man!" (2 Samuel 12:1-7)

David begged God for forgiveness, and while there would be a consequence for his actions, it was far milder than it could have been. I would think that God would take away David's kingdom, his palace, his money, his reputation, his family support, Bathsheba and his child.

But that's not what God did.

God took the baby they conceived in adultery.

David one, didn't go to war for his country; two, played the peeping-tom on a married woman; three, had sex with her; four, conceived an illegitimate child; five, tried to cover it up; and six, had an innocent man murdered.

At what point in the story did God finally enact punishment on David? It wasn't until the sixth sin that God finally said, enough is enough.

I don't know you, but I know that I have not done anything like what David did. God knows everything that I have ever said or done, and while I am not perfect, I do not deserve my child to be ripped away. Let's stop kidding ourselves that the pack of gum you stole when you were five makes your hard life a fitting punishment. If this is a trial then this is not a cause and effect event. You didn't cause it and God is not punishing you.

You aren't perfect. Ask God to forgive you, and then move on. A paraphrase of Psalm 103:11-17 from *The Message*, says:

> God makes everything come out right;
> he puts victims back on their feet.
> He showed Moses how he went about his work,
> opened up his plans to all Israel.
> God is sheer mercy and grace;
> not easily angered, he's rich in love.
> He doesn't endlessly nag and scold,
> nor hold grudges forever.
> He doesn't treat us as our sins deserve,
> nor pay us back in full for our wrongs.
> As high as heaven is over the earth,
> so strong is his love to those who fear him.
> And as far as sunrise is from sunset,
> he has separated us from our sins.
> As parents feel for their children,
> God feels for those who fear him.
> He knows us inside and out,
> keeps in mind that we're made of mud.
> Men and women don't live very long;
> like wildflowers they spring up and blossom,
> But a storm snuffs them out just as quickly,
> leaving nothing to show they were here.
> God's love, though, is ever and always,
> eternally present to all who fear him,

Don't let Satan lie to you. You are already broken, do not allow yourself to be defeated.

Force yourself to go to church every week. Read the Bible daily. Join a Bible study. You need to flex your spiritual muscles and show the Devil that he has no power over you. The Devil's goal is to separate you from God and from God's people. He wants to destroy you physically, spiritually and emotionally. Do not allow him to win.

If you can make it through this—and I'm living proof that you can—then you will emerge stronger than you ever thought possible.

There is a warrior deep inside of you, for heaven's sake, let it loose!

Listen to the talk, *How to Overcome the Devil part 1* at www.MarieWhiteAuthor.com. Go to the "Strength for Parents" tab and click Book Link 8.

Steps to remember:
- Sometimes you win and sometimes you learn
- Stop believing that you deserve this
- Release your inner warrior

CHAPTER 7

Giving it all Away

Some days I'm numb, just making it through the day. Other days I'm full of hope, waiting with bated breath for an email, call, or doorbell that says our child is coming home.

Like the prophet Hosea, whom God commanded to marry a prostitute, we have been entrusted with a hard task.

James MacDonald said, "By faith I can choose the future over the moment." We have to choose the future, because *this* moment is full of heartache.

Jesus said, "Blessed are those who mourn, for they shall be comforted" (Matthew 5:4).

I have to stop myself when I start to imagine what a changed person our child will be when they return, or when I try to imagine being given the worst news. I remind myself not to grieve before the grief. If the worst never happens, then I have grieved for nothing, and if it does, then the time for grieving will come. I don't need to do it twice.

There are several parallel storylines that are going on simultaneously while our child is missing. We can see some of the things that God is doing, and I can tell there are things that we know nothing about.

One storyline we see is that this is the enemy persecuting our family for being Christians. Another aspect is that our family is growing its spiritual muscles. Our faith is also being tested, so that we can learn to trust God no matter what the circumstances.

Experiencing a missing child has also led us to other ministry opportunities, new friendships, and the chance to love people we never would have known.

We are tasked with the assignment of bringing light into dark places and fighting for the future of a child who is worth all of this.

It's a privilege to be used by God in these ways. The Bible says that if we can stay strong, and persevere, then we will see a good result. God's timing is perfect.

> Let us not become weary in doing good, for at the proper time we will reap a harvest if we do not give up (Galatians 6:9).

I have searched the Bible, and listened to hundreds of Christian songs. Nowhere can I find a song that says to give up, take the easy way out, or to despair. Every verse says the opposite. Keep hoping, keep trying, keep straining on tiptoes to see past the horizon, to the good that God will make from this event.

There is evidence of the miraculous all around us.

Being brave isn't supposed to be easy. —Sam Berns

When life gets tough, have you found that family becomes even more precious to you? Do you feel that at any moment this could be the last time you see them? Are you beginning to wonder if God will take you through more struggles?

Sometimes I am filled with jealousy and anger over the thought that someone else has my child. I see families together and I cry out to God, "Why do they get to have their children and we have to go through *this*?" I want to grab each person by the shoulders and say that they need to savor every moment together.

There is an empty space in my heart that nothing can replace.

In those moments it is hardest to take every thought captive.

I whisper, "Lord, please use our pain for Your glory."

We have to fight the urge to become what we are fighting. This battle against evil is being disguised as something else. Maybe your battle seems to be against a person or an action, but the reality is that it is against evil, and that person is only a pawn.

You must fight against becoming bitter and taking it out on the people around you. Remind yourself of who it is you are fighting. The Bible says:

> Finally, be strong in the Lord and in his mighty power. Put on the full armor of God, so that you can take your stand against the devil's schemes. For our struggle is not against flesh and blood, but against the rulers, against the authorities, against the powers of this dark world and against the spiritual forces of evil in the heavenly realms. Therefore put on the full armor of God, so that when the day of evil comes, you may be able to stand your ground, and after you have done everything, to stand. Stand firm then, with the belt of truth buckled around your waist, with the breastplate of righteousness in place, and with your feet fitted with the readiness that comes from the gospel of peace. In addition to all this, take up the shield of faith, with which you can extinguish all the flaming arrows of the evil one. Take the helmet of salvation and the sword of the Spirit, which is the word of God. And pray in the Spirit on all occasions with all kinds of prayers and requests (Ephesians 6:10-18).

You are still here! Some days that will have to be enough. There are times when we feel like we are in a war and under "radio silence" as we wait for God to answer our prayers. In those times, keep praying for strength to make it through the day. I know that each minute seems to last an hour. Also, pray that the evil people in your life would have their hearts changed, and that God would vindicate you. "Vengeance is mine, saith The Lord" (Romans 12:19).

God's training program includes a lesson on learning to love the unlovable.

It is almost as if God is putting people in front of us and asking us to love them in spite of themselves. Can we love those who hate us? Can we love those who do not love themselves? Can we love those who hurt the ones we love?

> Don't take revenge, dear friends. Instead, let God's anger take care of it. After all, scripture says, "I alone have the right to take revenge. I will pay back, says the Lord" (Romans 12:19 ESV).

You and I wrestle with fear, guilt, jealousy, hopelessness, and the Jekyll and Hyde emotional rollercoaster of life. It all seems overwhelming. One day you want to give up, and the next day it feels like victory is right around the corner.

The one emotion that everyone rightly expects you to have is fear. What they don't realize is just how debilitating fear is. You cannot give in to the fear.

I remember how I felt those first few days.

Each time I made it through an hour, a whole day, or a phone call, and survived, I found out that I was stronger than I thought.

I used to wake up each morning look at the ceiling and say, "It's just you and me, Lord. Let's do this."

> And so seated next to my father in the train compartment, I suddenly asked, "Father, what is sexsin?" He turned to look at me, as he always did when answering a question, but to my surprise he said nothing. At last he stood up, lifted his traveling case off the seat and set it on the floor. "Will you carry it off the train, Corrie?" he said. I stood up and tugged at it. It was crammed with the watches and spare parts he had purchased that morning. "It's too heavy," I said. "Yes," he said, "and it would be a pretty poor father who would ask his little girl to carry such a load. It's the same way, Corrie, with knowledge. Some knowledge is too heavy for children. When you are older and stronger, you can bear it. For now you must trust me to carry it for you. —Corrie Ten Boom

Just like Corrie, you and I have to let God carry our burdens for us. We don't know the answers to all our questions yet, and trying to figure them out only makes us burn with anger and resentfulness. If we choose to trust God, then we need to trust His motives to be good and pure. Trust is a choice.

Like Moses, you can choose to trust.

In the story of the Exodus, Moses leaves for forty days. During those forty days, most of the people despaired, thinking that Moses had died. But, we need to put this in context. This was *after* God had given them the signs and wonders of the ten plagues. *After* God had provided water in the desert. *After* God had sent them bread from heaven. Yet here they are, going through forty days of silence, and all their trust in God is gone?

Which begs the question, was there any trust in Him to begin with? Did they only believe because they saw?

Before God performed these miracles, he told Moses that He would part the Red Sea and kill the Egyptians. So that, "The Egyptians will know that I am the Lord when I gain glory through Pharaoh, his chariots and his horsemen." (Exodus 14:18)

God *wanted* to show His glory.

If you are a Christian, then in your story and mine, God also wants to show His glory. I am willing to hold on until I see it. Are you?

> I don't think God trusts just anybody with so much heartache. The world has not yet seen what God can do with a man who gives both halves of a broken heart to him. And I don't doubt that a man like that can change the world ... or at least a little part of it.
> —Chris Fabry

God has already taken us through times of silence, where we had to depend on Him, and He has shown Himself faithful. Now, it's time for us to use those spiritual muscles to make it to the end of this journey.

We can do this!

Oh, who are we kidding? We can't do this.

But with God's strength we will.

Potato Sack Promises

Three days after our child was taken, I gave my body permission to throw up. I had felt like vomiting from day one, but it was such an odd response that I kept holding it back. I think that I viewed it as weakness. On day three, I suddenly realized that it was okay not to be okay.

Forget sleeping at night. I was devastated, hungry and filled with terror. It seemed like evil was all around me. I would try to pray all night while listening to audiobooks or sermons. I tried everything I could think of to stop my mind from racing and break free from the terror. Nothing worked.

As days became weeks and weeks became months, my body began to calm down.

However, a few months later an update on our child sent me into that same spiral. Adrenaline, cortisol, stomach knot, tension, and the feeling of evil all came rushing back.

But something had changed since the first few days, and I no longer gave in to those feelings. Within minutes the terror was gone.

I had changed.

I was no longer holding on to potato-sack promises.

Author Don McClure wrote about a funny email he received. It read:

> Begin by standing in your cubicle with a five-pound potato sack in each hand, then extend your arms straight out. Hold your arms out for one minute initially. Using the same technique, progress to ten-pound potato sacks after a week or two. Hold your arms out a little longer, as your strength increases. With time, you'll work up to twenty-five-pound potato sacks, then fifty-pound sacks, and then one day, just by repeating this exercise, you will actually be able to hold a one hundred-pound potato sack in each hand for a full minute. Once you've gotten to that level, start putting a few potatoes in the sacks and continue with the exercise routine.

Don goes on to explain that when we first encounter a problem, we cling to a verse such as Galatians 6:9 which says, "Let us not become weary in doing good, for at the proper time we will reap a harvest if we do not give up." At first it's an empty sack, "Sometimes it's all we can do to hold on to the sack, just the promise all by itself." Then he says that God, "gives somebody a verse that's empty, almost meaningless at the time it's given—beyond any hope or dream—and He moves them out like He did Abraham."

As we go through hard times God puts potatoes into our sack, one by one.

Then, as Abraham walks Isaac up the mountain he realizes, "God spent fifty years making Abraham equal to the promise...After fifty years of holding a potato sack that says one hundred pounds on the outside, it contains one hundred pounds on the inside—and he holds it!"

That is a beautiful illustration of what the inspiration cards at the back of this book have been to me. At first they seemed too good to be true.

You may ask:

Can God give me strength when I feel like giving up? (1 Peter 5:6-11)

Does God promise to deliver me? (Psalm 119:170b)

Will God answer me? (Psalm 120:1)

How can God answer us, or help us go on? It's not like a booming voice from the clouds is going to shake the house. Then a day comes when you can't imagine that you will make it another moment, and something miraculous happens. Not only do you keep going, but a friend says the exact answer to your unspoken prayer. The radio plays a special song you haven't heard in years. Words in the Bible jump off the page in answer to your most difficult decision. And your eyes fill with tears as you whisper, "You do answer."

We almost always find that there's a gap between God making a promise and God fulfilling it. That gap is there to develop our trust in Him.

In *Lord of the Rings*, Tolkien wrote, "I don't know how to say it, but after last night I feel different. I seem to see ahead, in a kind of way. I know we are going to take a very long road, into darkness; but I know I can't turn back."

God is strengthening you to make you equal to the task He has put before you.

Now take up your weapons, warrior, and let's press-on to the victory.

Steps to remember:
- Being brave isn't supposed to be easy
- Promises begin like empty sacks
- God will make you equal to the task

And we know that in all things God works for the good of those who love him, who have been called according to his purpose (Romans 8:28).

CHAPTER 8

Strength from Above

Weeks turned into months and our child was still not home, but life began to take on a new rhythm.

These are the things we learned:

1. You can still bounce back from crushing loss.
2. There is hope for a new normal.
3. You are stronger than you think, because you didn't think you could handle this, yet here you are.
4. "You can never learn that Christ is all you need, until Christ is all you have." —Corrie ten Boom
5. There is still joy in the midst of crushing pain, when you know God.
6. God is never closer than when you are hurting.
7. "God whispers in our pleasures, but shouts in our pain."— C.S. Lewis
8. You cannot give in to the enemy's lies.
9. God is faithful; He will not let you be tempted beyond what you can bear. But when you are tempted, He will also

provide a way out so that you can endure it (1 Corinthians 10:13).
10. God is real. God is trustworthy. God is good.

All rescues are from God, there may be a few days of silence, but keep holding on to Him.

> However, as it is written: "What no eye has seen, what no ear has heard, and what no human mind has conceived"— the things God has prepared for those who love him (1 Corinthians 2:9).

We are soldiers, and we have been given specific orders in this battle. This is the journey you and I are meant to take. We are supposed to live as though we are not afraid. We are supposed to bend, even when it doesn't seem fair. We are meant to fight for those who are weak, and speak up for them. In the process, we will find out how weak (or strong) our faith is. We will learn to keep our eyes focused on God alone.

This type of living was beautifully illustrated when Moses went to Pharaoh and said God wanted the Israelites to worship in the wilderness. Pharaoh said, "Who is the Lord, that I should obey him and let Israel go? I do not know the Lord and I will not let Israel go" (Exodus 5:2).

The Israelites had been Pharaoh's slaves for four-hundred years. Taking three days off should not be a problem. Even if they took a week, Pharaoh could have survived without them. But that was not Pharaoh's issue. His point was that these are *my* slaves, and I tell them what to do. How dare you come in here, and tell me what to do! I do not believe in your God, and I will not let them go.

The response was about Pharaoh's status, authority and pride. It's the same attitude we see from Satan, in the book of Job.

The people Moses had been sent to free lash out at him. In his confusion, Moses prays to God and says, "Why, Lord, why have you brought trouble on this people? Is this why you sent me? Ever since I went to Pharaoh to speak in your name, he has brought trouble on this people, and you have not rescued your people at all" (Exodus 5:22).

Do Moses' words sound familiar to you? How many times have we looked up and asked how God could allow another thing to go wrong in our lives? We want to say, "Is this why you sent me? You have not rescued me at all."

Like Moses, our story doesn't end at the point of God seeming to abandon us.

God instructs Moses to go back to Pharaoh, but not before God tells Moses "Now you will see what I will do to Pharaoh: Because of my mighty hand he will let them go…" (Exodus 6:1).

What will God do to Pharaoh in order to let the Israelites go? Will God terrify him in a dream? Will God strike Pharaoh with a bolt of lightning? Will God tell his people to revolt against the Egyptians?

Again, Moses goes before Pharaoh and tells him to let God's people go. Again, Pharaoh refuses.

God sends plague after plague on the Egyptians. Moses' brother Aaron stretches his staff over the water and it becomes blood. Aaron strikes the dust and it becomes gnats. Moses tells Pharaoh that if he does not let the Israelites go then the land would overflow with flies but the flies would only come to the Egyptians and their homes. The list goes on and on.

With each of these plagues, notice that it says, "Yet (Pharaoh's) heart was unyielding and he would not let the people go" (Exodus 9:7).

In the first few plagues it appears that perhaps Pharaoh hardened his own heart. But after a time, *God* hardened Pharaoh's heart. Did Pharaoh reach a point of no return?

The Bible has stories of rulers whom God forgave when they turned from their wicked ways and cried out to God for forgiveness. There seemed to be something different about Pharaoh.

One plague covered the people in sores (boils). There was a hail storm that killed the people and animals who were left outside (Exodus 9:18-26).

Even Pharaoh's officials began to fear God and start listening to Moses. They did what Moses said to do. But Pharaoh refused to listen (Exodus 9:20).

When the last plague came, it was the death of all the firstborn in the land of Egypt, *that* was the moment when Pharaoh finally let God's people go.

I think of Pharaoh as an illustration for the people who have our child. What if God is enacting hardship on their lives, until they let our child come home? What if they are covered in sores? How could God be afflicting them in order to force them to release their grip on our child? There are times when I'm ready to see some evidence of this and I shout at the ceiling, "All right, Lord, I'm ready to see some boils!"

> And we know that in all things God works for the good of those who love him, who have been called according to his purpose (Romans 8:28).

A New Normal

> A promise is the assurance that God gives to His people, so they can walk by faith, while they wait for Him to work.
> —James MacDonald

Right now, our house feels like an empty warehouse, but it has nothing to do with its size. While I don't walk from room to room, rubbing my hands across the walls and leaning against the doorjambs, my mind has done it a thousand times.

That is how I picture King David after his child with Bathsheba dies. Imagine an echoing palace, empty halls that resonate with the sobs of his grieving wife, and the constant cry of his aching heart. Did David grab a pillow in the night to scream into, open-mouthed, as shards of pain ripped through his body?

When the house is empty, I want to walk through it, touching things that my child touched, smelling things that smelled like my child: a pillow, a toy. It's been so long that the smell is gone.

David must have walked those halls, cool and dark in the night. Maybe it was the only time he could be alone, after spending all day running the affairs of the nation, and comforting his grieving wife. It could have been that night was when the grief crashed over him like waves that carried him deeper and deeper into an ocean of sadness.

Now I read the Bible with fresh eyes, bathed in pain. Job sits beside me, and we share pieces of pottery to scratch our oozing sores. Naomi, who asked to be called bitterness, sits with me in the car. Hosea, whom God asked to marry a prostitute, had to let betrayal into his heart so that he could show God's love to a wayward nation.

Now I understand the terrible gift Hosea was given.

> *Tribulations cannot cease until God either sees us remade or sees that our remaking is now hopeless.*
> –C.S. Lewis

Like Jonah was sent to his enemies, to tell them to ask God for forgiveness, we've been sent too. Like Esther, who would rather live quietly in the palace than risk her life, we would rather live a quiet life. We wait like King David, running for years, hiding in the wilderness, sleeping in caves, and holding on to the promise that God would one day make him king.

You and I can relate to all of them in some way.

Have you been falsely accused like Joseph? Or do you relate to the Hebrews in slavery, who thought God had abandoned them? Have you been discouraged like Paul, who "grieved to the point of death"? (2 Corinthians 1:8)

Job had to go through a horrible time of suffering. Yet, through all these tragedies, God had planned a great ending. Job suffered so that he could be an example to the devil. He demonstrated that no matter what Satan threw at us, if we truly trusted God, no one could take us away from God. How many lives did Job's suffering impact? He didn't just impact his contemporaries. Generations of lives after Job, even you and I, have been affected.

Through his story we also learn that after the trial, come the blessings. (Job 42:12-17)

I can only imagine what David was going through when he wrote Psalm 13. He was running from Saul's army, hiding in caves, and waiting for God to keep His promise when he wrote:

> *O Lord, how long will you forget me? Forever?*
> *How long will you look the other way?*
> *How long must I struggle with anguish in my soul,*
> *with sorrow in my heart every day?*
> *How long will my enemy have the upper hand?*
> *Turn and answer me, O Lord my God!*
> *Restore the sparkle to my eyes, or I will die.*
> *Don't let my enemies gloat, saying,*
> *"We have defeated him!"*
> *Don't let them rejoice at my downfall.*
> *But I trust in your unfailing love.*
> *I will rejoice because you have rescued me.*

> *I will sing to the Lord*
> *because he is good to me.*
> *–Psalm 13 NLT*

God is like that, predictably unpredictable.

When Jesus healed people, even of the same blindness, He did it in two different ways. It seems like Jesus didn't want us to fall into the trap of thinking that if we use a formula, then we will get results from God. There is no perfect prayer. Each miracle is unique. Each miracle, personalized.

If you are a Christian, then that is how you and I will be delivered from our ordeals.

Uniquely.

Personally.

In God's perfect timing.

Now we know how the people who wrote the book of Psalms felt when they asked for justice, for vengeance, and for mercy. You and I know what it feels like to be the underdog, the poor, and the needy. We experience longings we never knew we had, like for this nightmare to end, and for the day we will see heaven. Our hearts scream, "Come quickly Lord Jesus! Rescue us!"

I want the people who have hurt our child to be brought to justice, to face punishment, and maybe, just maybe, to let Jesus change them.

I found out something wonderful about going through all those emotions. Now, when I read Psalms, I laugh and cry with REAL emotion because I've crawled into the Psalmist's skin and know the raw brokenness that he is feeling.

I know that when Job says, "Though He slay me, still I will trust Him" (Job 13:15) he didn't say it with exhaustion and resignation. He said it while screaming at the sky. It reminds me of the moments when I've shaken my fist and said to no one in particular, "Even if you take everything from me, I will choose to trust God!"

I can relate to David, about to lose his son with Bathsheba, and every sin he's committed is replayed in the theater of his mind. He knows God has seen them all, and that it is against God alone that he has sinned.

I have wanted to give-up a million times, so the pain of hoping would go away and we would just be left with the dull ache of defeat.

But, we have to hold on to God's promise to work things out for good.

God is never ever done.

Steps to remember:
- Your story is not over.
- A promise is the assurance that God gives to His people, so they can walk by faith while they wait for Him to work.
- We are waiting to see the end of the story.
- There is a new normal.
- You are stronger than you think.

And we know that in all things God works for the good of those who love him, who have been called according to his purpose (Romans 8:28).

CHAPTER 9

The Super Chicken

World famous author Beth Moore experienced a child missing from her life. In her Bible study, *The Patriarchs*, she wrote about the cupbearer forgetting Joseph in prison saying, "God won't waste a moment of the meantime to build Joseph into the kind of man his destiny demands" (Genesis 40:1-23). Beth knows what she is talking about.

That is incredibly powerful, especially when you think of it regarding your circumstances. It begs the question, what destiny is God preparing you to face?

> God often gives us a promise long before it could ever be true.
> —Don McClure

God had plenty of opportunities for Sarah and Abraham to have the promised son, still His answer to Sarah's prayers was not that she couldn't have a child, but that she couldn't have a child *yet*. God waited until Sarah and Abraham were at the right spiritual maturity to receive the blessing of their son Isaac. He also waited until they were past a point of physical ability, to make it miraculous (Genesis 17, 18, 21).

We are waiting on the miraculous.

We are waiting for God to make us into the people we were always meant to be. We are waiting to become the giants of the faith that God sees in us.

When God first spoke to Gideon, Gideon was hiding in a winepress. The first words to him were, "The Lord is with you, mighty warrior." Gideon was confused, there was nothing brave, mighty or warrior-ish about him.

God didn't see Gideon as he was, but as he would be. It wasn't long before God used Gideon to defeat the country's enemies.

> Right now, you're a Gideon. Right now, you're afraid, but one day you're going to lead troops into battle.
> –Greg Laurie

God has a special message for you and I, it's that we were made for a purpose. We have nothing to fear because God is with us, and He will work this out to make something good.

> *But now, this is what the Lord says—*
> *he who created you, Jacob,*
> *he who formed you, Israel:*
> *"Do not fear, for I have redeemed you;*
> *I have summoned you by name; you are mine.*
> *When you pass through the waters,*
> *I will be with you;*
> *and when you pass through the rivers,*
> *they will not sweep over you.*
> *When you walk through the fire,*
> *you will not be burned;*
> *the flames will not set you ablaze.*
> *For I am the Lord your God,*
> *the Holy One of Israel, your Savior.*
> —Isaiah 43:1-7

WAITING

We are still waiting.

Whenever we take our eyes off God and only look at our circumstances, we are setting ourselves up for heartbreak. We are decorating for a pity party.

God knows where you are. He also knows which spiritual muscles you will need in the future and He has become your personal trainer.

I feel like God has handed me this cup of hardship and said, "Can I trust you with this?"

I answer, "No. No, Lord, you can't." Then I change my answer to, "Okay, but I don't like this cup." Later, it becomes, "Yes, I will carry it, but it's too hard." Finally, I hand it back to Him, saying, "Only you can carry it, Lord."

> Have I not commanded you? Be strong and courageous. Do not be afraid; do not be discouraged, for the Lord your God will be with you wherever you go (Joshua 1:9).

When God started walking me through the decision to trust Him, my first step was to make weekend plans. Only those who have been through the same type of thing can fully comprehend what a big deal that was. Could I trust God to bring our child home, even if I wasn't waiting by the window? But something strange began to happen; as I started to trust Him, I began to let go. My hands started to unclench. My shoulders relaxed. All the weight I had been carrying was now on God's shoulders, where it should have been all along.

Reading my Bible study that talked about making money, status, family, work or achievements into idols made me ask, could I trust God instead of fixating on my missing child? It was a big step for me and a baby step toward handing this over to God.

It wasn't easy and it didn't happen overnight, but I slowly handed our missing child to God. And He proved Himself worthy of my trust. As Joni Eareckson Tada said, "Never, never underestimate the ability of our God to use the shakiest prayer of the weakest saint to move heaven and earth."

> And Satan trembles when he sees, the weakest saint upon his knees. —William Cowper

In Joel 2:25-27 God promises His people that what they have lost will be repaid. He says, "I will repay you for the years the locusts have eaten ... and you will praise the name of the Lord your God, who has worked wonders for you; never again will my people be shamed. Then you will know that I am in Israel, that I am the Lord your God, and that there is no other; never again will my people be shamed."

God can take the time that has been gobbled-up and miraculously restore it. He can "repay you for the years that the locust have eaten." He can take that decimated heart of yours and make it into a spring of joy. He can make all things new.

How many times have you been put to shame? Maybe someone said that you deserved this. Did someone say that worse things happen to people? Or could it be that no one has said anything, but you are ashamed of yourself for not doing enough? Twice in that verse it says, "never again will my people be shamed." I look forward to that day, the day when this is behind us, and we will never again have reason for shame.

How many times have you imagined getting bad news and collapsing? You didn't think that you would be able to handle this. But, the phone would ring with another problem and you didn't collapse; something else went wrong and you handled it, and moved on.

Incredible.

Who knew?

> I realized that the deepest spiritual lessons are not learned by His letting us have our way in the end, but by His making us wait, bearing with us in love and patience until we are able to honestly pray what He taught His disciples to pray: Thy will be done.
> —Elisabeth Elliot

Give yourself the freedom to hope and plan for God to make a way in your situation.

Psalm 61 announces "The Year of the Lord's Favor," a special time when wrongs are made right. I could explain each line, but instead I will let you read it for yourself. You will want to get a marker and highlight your favorite parts. Are you waiting for a captive to be released? Highlight that line. Are you waiting for vengeance on your enemies? Mark that in bright yellow. Do you want God to renew your ruined family? It says that He will "bestow on them a crown of beauty instead of ashes, the oil of joy instead of mourning." You and I can't wait until the day we have joy instead of ashes.

> *Of one thing I am perfectly sure:*
> *God's story never ends with ashes.*
> —Elisabeth Elliot

Even though you can't see it right now, God is at work. This article by Stephen Altrogge, is called *All the Things God is Doing When it Looks Like He is Doing Nothing.* Read it at tinyurl.com/lgqwhdz or at the Strength for Parents tab at MarieWhiteAuthor.com.

God is good. All the time. And He is not done with us yet. He is still at work.

Steps to remember:
- God can make you into the person you were always meant to be.
- The time that has been lost can be repaid.
- God's story never ends with ashes.

And we know that in all things God works for the good of those who love him, who have been called according to his purpose (Romans 8:28).

CHAPTER 10

When Your Pain is the Gift

Fear. Who could have imagined? Just when it felt like the battle would be won, fear came out of nowhere. What if getting our child back is not as great as we expect? What if our child is not the same?

What if?

What if?

Fear does not come from God. He specifically says in His word, "do what is right and do not give way to fear" (1 Peter 3:6) and again, "Do not be anxious about anything, but in every situation, by prayer and petition, with thanksgiving, present your requests to God. And the peace of God, which transcends all understanding, will guard your hearts and your minds in Christ Jesus" (Philippians 4:6-7). "For God has not given us a spirit of fear, but of power and of love and of a sound mind" (2 Timothy 1:7 NKJV).

Who could have predicted that a shot of fear would come right when victory was in sight? Obviously, this was a spiritual attack. I would love to say that the enemy could never beat me, but that would be a lie. I am weak, but God is strong. With God, nothing can beat us.

There have been days when I felt invincible! On those days, I wanted to beat my chest like Tarzan and yell, "I will not be afraid!" That's how we should live every day, but usually we don't.

Even Paul, the super-Christian, had times were life was more than he could handle. He wondered if he would even survive those times. Paul felt tremendous spiritual oppression. The word oppress can also mean to wear down[3]. You know that pressure, when it feels like you are in a vise, about to pop.

Paul wrote:

> We do not want you to be uninformed, brothers and sisters, about the troubles we experienced in the province of Asia. We were under great pressure, far beyond our ability to endure, so that we despaired of life itself. Indeed, we felt we had received the sentence of death. But this happened that we might not rely on ourselves but on God, who raises the dead. He has delivered us from such a deadly peril, and he will deliver us again. On him we have set our hope that he will continue to deliver us, as you help us by your prayers. Then many will give thanks on our behalf for the gracious favor granted us in answer to the prayers of many (2 Corinthians 1:8-11).

God has not left us in the dark.

His timing is in everything. I can almost see myself looking back on this in the future and seeing that this was the time when we felt most alive. When living meant something, and that one day we will see what the purpose was for all this pain.

> How do I live in the world I have with my woundedness? How do I live as an alive woman in the world I have? I've been crying and it just keeps going ... but it's oh so good, because it is also a feeling of being alive. —*The Journey of Desire*

Sometimes I'm tempted to say, "Really, God? Why haven't you rescued our child? Where are you? Why won't you save us? Do you even care?"

Then I remember what C.S. Lewis said about waiting on God:

A faint analogy would be this. It is one thing to ask in vacua whether So-and-So will join us tonight, and another to discuss this when So-and-So's honour is pledged to come and some great matter depends on his coming. In the first case it would be merely reasonable, as the clock ticked on, to expect him less and less. In the second, a continued expectation far into the night would be due to our friend's character if we had found him reliable before. Which of us would not feel slightly ashamed if, one moment after we had given him up, he arrived with a full explanation of his delay? We should feel that we ought to have known him better.

We do know Him better. It would be easy to be angry at God and looking at our innocence say, "And this is our reward?" But that is not true.

This isn't the end of our story.

Only God knows how this is all going to end. I know that in the end we will echo Lewis' sentiments that we should have known better. God is for us. Who can be against us?

One day we will say, like King Solomon:

> See! The winter is past;
> the rains are over and gone.
> Flowers appear on the earth;
> the season of singing has come.
> —Song of Songs 2:11-12

As time progresses, you will find that something has changed in you. You are no longer the person you were. You won't respond to things that scared you in the same way that you used to. When something happens, you'll want to cry, but you won't. You will want to get stressed-out about something, but instead you will wait to see if things will change. You will have turned into a person with patience.

> Be joyful in hope, patient in affliction,
> faithful in prayer (Romans 12:12).

You will start to see yourself becoming stronger. You'll start to notice that there are potatoes in the empty sacks you've been carrying.

> Outside the will of God there is nothing I want, and in the will of
> God there is nothing I fear. —A.W. Tozer

Somewhere down the line there is still light at the end of the tunnel. Trust God and believe that He is still orchestrating your life toward some grand outcome, even when it feels impossible.

There are a few ways that you can show God's power over your life. They are:

1. To show unceasing devotion to God, regardless of what He has allowed.
2. To have unwavering trust in God, even when you can't see any way that He could make success out of your situation.
3. To be an unbelievably bright light, shining God's love on everyone you meet.
4. To have an unending grip on God's promises, like Jacob said to the angel he wrestled, "I won't let go until you bless me!" (Genesis 32:26)

Stand with me, as Gandalf stood before the flames of Balrog, and let us tell the devil that he can't take another inch of ground in our lives. Scream at him that your house belongs to God and that he, "shall NOT pass!"

> But even if you should suffer for what is right, you are blessed. "Do not fear their threats; do not be frightened." But in your hearts revere Christ as Lord. Always be prepared to give an answer to everyone who asks you to give the reason for the hope that you have. But do this with gentleness and respect, keeping a clear conscience, so that those who speak maliciously against your good behavior in Christ may be ashamed of their slander. For it is better, if it is God's will, to suffer for doing good than for doing evil (1 Peter 3:14-17).

In the middle of your journey, thank God. Trust Him. Trust that He has your best interest at heart and let it go.

When you feel like you have nowhere to go, give your problem to God and let Him do what you can't.

Fear

When you are deep in the battle, do not give in to despair or hopelessness.

> the Lord knows how to rescue the godly from trials
> —2 Peter 2:9

What happens when everyone around you gives up on your hope for a brighter future?

People try to save our family from additional pain by telling us that it may not be God's will to bring our child home, as if we had not already thought of that.

When Greg Laurie experienced the death of his son he was told; "You need to get over this," "When life gives you lemons, make lemonade," and "What doesn't kill you makes you stronger."

The pain of losing a child is hard enough without these insensitive comments. If I could go back in time I would have sent an email to friends that said, "In your effort to console us, please do not share anything that is negative. Each day our minds are bombarded by a thousand horrific scenarios that make us want to roll into the fetal position and convulse with fear. The last thing we need is for someone to come up to us and confront us with our worst fears. We know that you only want to be there for us, and make us aware of any scenario that we may not have thought of. Believe me, we've thought of the good, the bad, and the devastating. If you want to help us, pray with us when you see us, give us an encouraging verse, tell us that you are praying for our child, drop us a note or text. We value your love and compassion, and we don't want to go through this alone."

Take the time to ask other people what they are struggling with.

They are carrying burdens too. While they may not be as bad as what yours, you will find that as you start to pray for others, your problems won't seem nearly as overwhelming. As you pray for them, you will connect with them in a special way. The next time you see a friend, ask them how their struggle is going? Tell them that you've been praying for them. When you are feeling sorry for yourself, the best thing you can do is reach out to others. While their pain may not be the same as yours, sometimes you may feel grateful that you are "only" going through this and not what they are going through.

What do you wish someone would do for you right now? Do it for someone else.

If you've never heard of her, Joni Eareckson Tada is a famous speaker, author and painter. She is also a quadriplegic, paralyzed from the neck down. Joni wasn't born that way. She had an accident when she was a teenager. When she realized that she would be an invalid for the rest of her life, she wanted to die, but God stepped in and held her in His arms.

When I think of our child and how terrible it is to be without them, I can't help but think of Joni. I know that she would have been grateful to have been a mom, even for a little while. What she would have given for the ability to wrap her arms around a child and feel the bond that many of us have been privileged to experience.

Instead Joni has lived more than forty years bound to a wheelchair, in excruciating physical pain. She has known physical and emotional pain beyond what I can imagine. I wouldn't trade my situation for hers.

Joni doesn't give up. She praises God through it all and has led many other people to Jesus. She learned to paint by holding the brush in her teeth. She has written many books. She has spoken all around the world and she has helped thousands of people. She has the attitude that you and I need to have, "You can't beat me, devil. I may be weak, but God is strong!"

> When Christ gives us strength to tackle a painful situation, gaining contentment doesn't mean losing sorrow or saying good-bye to discomfort. You can be sorrowful yet always rejoicing. You can have nothing and yet possess everything. First Timothy 6:6 says, "Godliness with contentment is great gain." Yet the gain always comes through loss. The grace always comes through need. Don't let anyone tell you that contentment comes easily. It is not passive.

> In fact, it is gritty determination. It has to be learned. And it requires grace from beyond this world. —Joni Eareckson Tada

If anyone should have given up, it's Joni. Instead she became a beacon of light, shining in the darkness. We all face darkness in some form.

Christian faith is not the blissful, pie-in-the-sky feeling of "I wish." Faith is trust in God.

Each of us has someone in our lives that we can trust to do what they say they will do. Faith is trusting that when we can't see what God is doing, He is still doing something that will be for our good.

> Now faith is the substance of things hoped for, the evidence of things not seen. —Hebrews 11:1 KJ21

> When a train goes through a tunnel and it gets dark, you don't throw away the ticket and jump off. You sit still and trust the engineer. —Corrie Ten Boom

Faith is trusting the God that we know and the promises that He has made. We have to trust that He will not disappoint us.

C.S. Lewis' tongue-in-cheek statement explains the reality of trust, "We're not necessarily doubting that God will do the best for us; we are wondering how painful the best will turn out to be."

Some of us know how painful the best has been. What I had to decide ahead of time was that even if our child did not come home, it would not break my trust in God.

We can't allow our circumstances to define us. Like a caterpillar emerging as a butterfly, like muscle is made by being torn and repairing itself, so our walk with Jesus is born from suffering.

We are not the same people we were at the beginning of this journey.

Would I want to go back to being the person I once was? I would take the naiveté of thinking that the world is a nice place and that people are inherently good, but how would I relate to people who went through suffering? Would I always assume that they played some part in the blame? Would I tell them that God would never let anything bad happen? Would I scoff at injustice as though it didn't exist? Would I question God's sovereignty when others were going through unthinkable circumstances?

Yes. I would.

We are growing, and growth is painful.

Finding God in the midst of the pain is a gift beyond measure. In the movie, *The Nativity Story* Mary and Joseph stop to warm themselves by a fire. They talk to a shepherd and he says, "we are all given a gift," implying that Mary's baby is her gift. He has no idea that she is carrying the son of God, and what a nightmare being unwed and pregnant has been for them.

What if you and I find out that our trials *are* the gift?

Pastor Saeed knew this when he wrote this Christmas letter from inside a cold, Iranian prison. He spent years imprisoned, away from his wife and young children, yet he writes with the joy that can only come from hardship.

> RajaiShahr Prison, 2014
>
> Merry Christmas! These days are very cold here. My small space beside the window is without glass making most nights unbearable to sleep. The treatment by fellow prisoners is also quite cold and at times hostile. Some of my fellow prisoners don't like me because I am a convert and a pastor. They look at me with shame as someone who has betrayed his former religion...
>
> Today we like (Jesus) should come out of our safe comfort zone in order to proclaim the Word of Life and Salvation though faith in Jesus Christ and the penalty of sin that He paid on the cross and to proclaim His resurrection. We should be able to tolerate the cold, the difficulties and the shame in order to serve God. We should be able to enter into the pain of the cold dark world. Then we are able to give the fiery love of Christ to the cold wintery manger of those who are spiritually dead. It might be necessary to come out of the comfort of our lives and leave the loving embrace of our family to enter the manger of the lives of others, such as it has been for me for the third consecutive Christmas. It may be that we will be called fools and traitors and face many difficulties, but we should crucify our will and wishes even more until the world hears and tastes the true meaning of Christmas.

> Christmas means that God came so that He would enter your hearts today and transform your lives and to replace your pain with indescribable joy...
>
> Christmas is the day that the heat of the life-giving fire of God's love shone in the dark cold wintry frozen hearts and burst forth in this deadly wicked world...
>
> So this Christmas let the lava-like love of Christ enter into the depth of your heart and make you fiery, ready to pay any cost in order to bring the same lava love to the cold world around you, transforming them with the true message of Christmas.
>
> Pastor Saeed Abedini
> Soaking in the lava love of Christ

Until you have lived it, you cannot know how much God shows up in pain. He is real, and He is good.

> Not only so, but we also glory in our sufferings, because we know that suffering produces perseverance; perseverance, character; and character, hope. —Romans 5:3-4

There are three books I recommend, that will give you a perspective change.

#1- *The Prayer of Jabez*, by Bruce Wilkinson
#2- *This Present Darkness*, by Frank Peretti
#3- *The Hiding Place*, by Corrie Ten Boom

Each of these books reminds me that in the end, evil always loses. You and I need to remember that daily, because in our lives it seems like evil has won. *The Prayer of Jabez* helps you to understand your purpose. *This Present Darkness* gives you a picture of the spiritual battle you are fighting. *The Hiding Place* shows you how to have faith when all seems lost.

If you are a Christian, then each day you fight a dozen little battles. When you choose to drag yourself to church, to Bible study, to pray or spend time with another Christian; these are small victories. The enemy does not want you to battle on your knees. Every time you have a headache, feel sick, are too tired or any of a thousand different excuses, yet you persevere and go to church anyway, you have fought and won. Every small victory is an inch closer to evil's fatal blow.

When Job had everything taken from him, he chose to praise God and say "The Lord gave and the Lord has taken away; may the name of the Lord be praised." In that moment, he gained ground. Job won a decisive battle when he was told to curse God and die but instead said, "Shall we accept good from God, and not trouble?" When his friends blamed him for his own misfortune he hung on to the truth as he said, "I will never admit you are in the right; till I die, I will not deny my integrity" (Job 27:5).

It's hard to hold on to truth and easy to believe the lies.

Do you fear that there's something hidden in your heart that needs to be weeded out?

It's fine to ask God to examine your heart, as long as you don't give in to the lies. You have to cling to God and like Job say, "But he knows the way that I take; when he has tested me, I will come forth as gold." Job 23:10

> I read the paper every day and the Bible every day; that way I know what both sides are up to. —Zig Ziglar

In *The Lord of the Rings*, Tolkien wrote, "The quest stands upon the edge of a knife. Stray but a little and it will fail, to the ruin of all. Yet hope remains, while company is true. Do not let your hearts be troubled."

Tolkien was paraphrasing Jesus who said, "Don't let your hearts be troubled. Trust in God, and trust in me" (John 14:1 NCV).

When you pray for strength, guidance and faith, you can approach each day with the confidence that you have done all that God has asked of you. The rest of the story is up to Him.

He is not done with you yet.

For our family, we are not the same people we were. We are already changed. Healing has happened and growth on a monumental scale. We have learned that growth is painful, but pain is temporary, and eternity is worthwhile. In the meantime, we wait for the promises in the verse below.

> *All who rage against you*
> *will surely be ashamed and disgraced;*
> *those who oppose you*
> *will be as nothing and perish.*
> *Though you search for your enemies,*
> *you will not find them.*
> *Those who wage war against you*
> *will be as nothing at all.*
> *For I am the Lord your God*
> *who takes hold of your right hand*
> *and says to you, do not fear;*
> *I will help you.* —Isaiah 41:11-13

Chosen

What if God chose you and I for this very moment? What if He chose us just like He chose Abraham to start a nation, Moses to lead a people, David to rule a country and John the Baptist to prepare the coming of Jesus. In every generation there are a few chosen people whom God uses in a mighty way. What if we are those chosen people, chosen to display His goodness in the middle of our adversity.

> We are supposed to show the superiority of the life lived in Christ. That's why Christians get cancer. That's why Christian parents have prodigals. —James MacDonald

The story of Joseph and the story of Esther both illustrate God's rigorous training program for those He plans to place in the spotlight.

Joseph's training began when he chose to serve his master faithfully in the midst of pain. It happened again when he faithfully served his jailer in the midst of injustice. These experiences were both preparing him for his calling in life, second in command over all of Egypt. He was then able to save the people of Egypt and his own people of Israel.

In the end, Joseph tells his brothers that what they intended for evil, God intended for good (Genesis 37.)

The Bible gives ample warning that as Christians, we should expect problems to arise, because we are God's children. It also says to have peace and stand firm because something better is coming.

Jesus said:
- I have told you these things, so that in me you may have peace. In this world you will have trouble. But take heart! I have overcome the world" (John 16:33).
- You will be hated by everyone because of me, but the one who stands firm to the end will be saved" (Matthew 10:22).
- Blessed are you when people hate you, when they exclude you and insult you and reject your name as evil, because of the Son of Man" (Luke 6:22).

I don't think that Jesus meant that we would only be blessed in heaven. In Psalm 27 the psalmist says that he is confident that he will see God's goodness "in the land of the living," meaning here on Earth, not just in heaven. Psalm 27:12-14 reads, "Do not turn me over to the desire of my foes, for false witnesses rise up against me, spouting malicious accusations. I remain confident of this: I will see the goodness of the Lord in the land of the living. Wait for the Lord; be strong and take heart and wait for the Lord."

The psalmist who wrote that is doing exactly what we talked about, giving thanks and trusting God **now**, before the good outcome has happened.

When you are going through hard things you need to praise God *before* the victory.

We learn about King Jehoshaphat in 2 Chronicles chapter 20. The king's people were up against several nations who wanted to destroy them. King Jehoshaphat chose to cry out to God for help instead of calling on another country to aid them. The king gathered all the people together to pray. Then, God answered them! When Jehoshaphat heard that God would defeat his enemies without a fight, he "appointed men to sing to the Lord and praise him for the splendor of his holiness…saying: 'Give thanks to the Lord, for his love endures forever'" (2 Chronicles 20:21).

And in Psalms we see, "We will not hide them from their descendants; we will tell the next generation the praiseworthy deeds of the Lord, his power, and the wonders he has done" (Psalm 78:4).

We are supposed to be grateful for every good thing, give God the gift of praise, and thank Him before we see the end result.

> Prayers will be answered in a way that brings God the most glory—and ultimate good to our lives…Yet it is usually strange answers to prayer that hide the deepest, best and most beautiful purposes.
> —Joni Eareckson Tada

Steps to remember:
- Growth is painful
- What do you wish someone would do for you?
- Do it for someone else
- We hear God the loudest when we are hurting

And we know that in all things God works for the good of those who love him, who have been called according to his purpose (Romans 8:28).

CHAPTER 11

They Can't Steal Your Joy

The two most important days in your life are the day you were born, and the day you find out why. –Mark Twain

God could be orchestrating something very special in your life. Your story is not over yet, not even close.

Sometimes I seem to catch a glimpse of what God is doing. After all, who else has gone through the life events that you and I have gone through, to prepare us for this exact moment?

Who else has the same perseverance?

Has God put you through the perfect training program, to equip you for what you are attempting?

> This is what the past is for! Every experience God gives us, every person He puts in our lives is the perfect preparation for the future that only He can see. –Corrie Ten Boom

Hardship should make you keenly aware of those around you who walk around with sadness in their eyes. If you haven't found them already, start looking for them. They are in your path for a reason.

It seems strange to say that you are in a battle, but it's true. At any point, you could throw in the towel and say that you can't do this anymore. You can't hope anymore, it hurts too much. You can't wait anymore, it's too stressful. You can't fight anymore, it's too dangerous.

The bottom line is that you can't go on like this, but if you ask God for strength, you will make it through.

When the enemy is bombarding me with lies, I remember that Jesus already has the victory. The enemy is just a spoiled child, throwing a fit because he can't get his way. He is not going to win. God will only let him go so far, and no further.

> There is no wisdom, no insight, no plan that can succeed against the Lord. The horse is made ready for the day of battle, but victory rests with the Lord. —Proverbs 21:30-3

John Eldridge wrote:

> This is precisely what the Bible (and all the stories that echo it) has warned us about all these years: we live in two worlds–or in one world with two halves, part that we can see and part that we cannot. We are urged, for our own welfare, to act as though the unseen world (the rest of reality) is, in fact, more weighty and more real and more dangerous than the part of reality we can see.

In my life, it has been obvious that God was using this event to unify my church, form relationships that will outlast each of the things we face, and bring more people to know Him.

> I could well believe that it is God's intention, since we have refused milder remedies, to compel us into unity, by persecution even and hardship. —C.S. Lewis

As C.S. Lewis said, "we touch upon the very central region where all doubts about our religion live. Things do look so very much as if our whole faith were a substitute for the real well-being we have failed to achieve on earth ... After all, we do not usually think much about the next world till our hopes in this have been pretty well flattened out..."

We look for God, when we do not understand what He is doing.

The enemy is crafty and he often uses those around us to speak the words we hope not to hear.

When we doubt our value, they tell us that we are worthless.

When we doubt our strength, they tell us that we are weak.

When we doubt our motives, they poke a finger into the soft spot in our armor and tell us that our selfish inclinations are the motivating factors.

We can't listen to the lies.

You need to doubt your doubts and believe your beliefs.

Only God can take this pile of scrambled lives and make them right again.

> Sir, my concern is not whether God is on our side; my greatest concern is to be on God's side, for God is always right.
> —Abraham Lincoln

> Never be afraid to trust an unknown future to a known God.
> —Corrie Ten Boom

STANDING STRONG

Sometimes I lift my chin like a willful child and do something to spite the devil. I put a garden sign in my front yard that reads, "This house is thankful." I don't do it with meekness and peace, I plant it like a flag on foreign territory. "Take that, devil." I think as I stab it into the ground.

I stubbornly refuse to allow evil to take my joy.

Make up your mind to beat this circumstance. Do not let doubt and fear define you.

Put notes of encouragement on your refrigerator, on your bathroom mirror, in your car, on your desk, at your computer. Sometimes those notes are the only thing that stands between you and despair.

Turn to the back of the book to the inspiration cards. Cut out and tape them in places you will see during the day.

There are days when I glare, defiantly, like a boxer taunting his opponent and say, "You will not defeat me, devil. We will be victorious. You have no power here and this house is THANKFUL! You think you can take me? You have no idea who you are up against. I may be weak, but you've picked on a child of the most high God. He will defeat you and He will use me to do it." I thumb my nose at the evil and I feel invincible, because I know who has my back.

God cannot be defeated.

> But the eyes of the Lord
> are on those who fear him,
> on those whose hope
> is in His unfailing love,
> to deliver them from death
> and keep them alive in famine.
> We wait in hope for the Lord;
> he is our help and our shield.
> In him our hearts rejoice,
> for we trust in His holy name.
> —Psalm 33:18-20

FOREVER CHANGED

I am not the same person that I used to be.

If there's one lesson that I've learned over the past few years, it's that God can be trusted. If He wants our child to come home, then He will make a way.

God knows what we need before we do. There will be times when you will feel like everything is against you. Things will go from bad to worst and just when you think it's over, something else goes wrong. But it doesn't last forever. There does come a day when things begin to work out. Things will get better and then things will be good again. The sun will break through the clouds.

In Exodus the people didn't want to follow Moses and frankly, Moses didn't want to lead them. The people start to complain. When they finally leave their Egyptian captors, the Israelites are a little cocky, strutting out of town. Only a few hours later, when they find out the Egyptian army is chasing them, they go from cocky to terrified. They panic and turn against Moses.

Things seem to go from bad to worse.

It was the same with the pilgrims.

First, they try to worship God in secret as they experience persecution from the king of England. Next, they leave the country, but they get caught. They are stripped and imprisoned. When trying to leave again, their wives and children are stranded at sea and the men get caught in a deadly storm. It takes a year before they are reunited in Amsterdam.

They start a printing press, only to have the king of England send soldiers over to Amsterdam to destroy it. They decide to go back to England and hire two ships to take them to America, but one of the ships breaks.

Could anything else possibly go wrong?

Half of them make it to America, and as soon as they arrive they begin to die by the dozens!

Good grief!

The end result of Moses leading the people out of Egypt, is victory. They make it across the Red Sea by walking on dry ground, and they gain freedom! The end of the Pilgrim's story is that a new nation is founded on Christian principles, and it becomes the most powerful nation on earth. From both horrible beginnings, come wonderful victories.

God was leading both Moses and the pilgrims, and it was the knowledge that they were in God's will, that made them persevere when others would have given up.

I am sure that the Israelites and the pilgrims both had days when they woke-up elated to be used in God's service. I'm sure that there were also days when they felt abandoned.

The fact that some of us will have good days at all, is a miracle. The fact that the bad days have not crushed us is a miracle too.

> Let us not become weary in doing good, for at the proper time we will reap a harvest if we do not give up (Galatians 6:9).

How many years did each person in the Bible wait before being rescued by God? Some waited a few years, others waited decades.

One thing they have in common is that God always showed up, because He is beautiful and He is faithful. They persevered through injustices, false accusations, uncertainty, hate and hardship, that continued until God fulfilled His plan for each of them, and the outcomes were incredible.

Family Problems

I am proof that God can make something beautiful from a horrible event. Five months into our child being gone, I became an online missionary, I started writing and created the popular YouTube channel *Bible Stories for Adults*. As I write this, four of my seven books have become Amazon best-sellers and those videos have been viewed over half a million times by people all around the world.

The funny scene I imagine is the enemy snickering and thinking to himself, "Ha. I have crushed them! They will never again be useful in God's kingdom."

Meanwhile, God is looking down and hides a little smile as He whispers, "No. You just wiped out any distractions so that they could accomplish my purposes."

Checkmate.

> God is with you. Rest. You are not alone. —Tony Evans

Elisabeth Elliot said, "The fact that I am a woman does not make me a different kind of Christian, but the fact that I am a Christian makes me a different kind of woman."

If you're a Christian, I mean a committed, read your Bible, look for ways to share Christ with others, living your life on-fire for God, kind of believer, then there are special implications for you in your struggle. As Jesus said, "If the world hates you, keep in mind that it hated me first" (John 15:18).

There are so many things in your future that you don't know yet, things God has planned, that you are unaware of. You may wonder why bad things happen to you. Meanwhile, you wait impatiently for miracles.

Miracles could be coming and they could be big.

Elisabeth Elliot's husband flew to Ecuador to tell an isolated tribe about Jesus. He and all his companions were killed just after they landed. How could that have happened? Weren't they going there to do God's work?

Elisabeth had so many questions for God when her husband's brutal death occurred. But that one tragic event caused an outpouring of Christ-like love in people's hearts. People flooded into Ecuador to share Jesus with that tribe. The tribe members became Christians. Even Elisabeth and her children went to visit the tribe in Ecuador.

There is no way that Elisabeth could have known what her husband's legacy would be, especially when it seemed like his mission was over.

God had something greater in mind, and it was greater than she or her husband could ever have fathomed.

She wrote, "If we hold tightly to anything given to us, unwilling to allow it to be used as the Giver means it to be used, we stunt the growth of the soul. What God gives us is not necessarily 'ours' but only ours to offer back to him, ours to relinquish, ours to lose, ours to let go of, if we want to be our true selves. Many deaths must go into reaching our maturity in Christ, many letting goes."

Here is the faith final exam as laid out by James MacDonald.

1. Do you believe that God is in control?
2. Do you believe that God is good?
3. Are you willing to wait —by faith— until the darkness becomes light?

Please look at these parts of the Bible and see if they apply to you: 1 Peter 5:6-11, Lamentations 3, Psalm 69, Psalm 24, Psalm 25, Psalm 40, and Psalm 119:81-88.

Steps to remember:
- You are fighting a battle.
- You can't win alone.

- Every part of your history has prepared you for this moment.
- You were made for a purpose.
- Bad times don't guarantee a bad ending.
- Wait until the darkness becomes light.

And we know that in all things God works for the good of those who love him, who have been called according to his purpose (Romans 8:28).

CHAPTER 12

The Final Curtain

As the heavens are higher than the earth, so are my ways higher than your ways and my thoughts than your thoughts. —Isaiah 55:9

Life is hard. There will be times when you spend days crying. You won't understand what God is doing and why God is not rescuing you from hardship. The money has run out and you are at a loss for what to do next. Fear reigns supreme in your life.

I look at the sky, my eyes filled with tears and want to scream, "Lord, do you love me so little, to put me through this?"

But, I know that it's not true. God loves us more than we could ever realize.

> Faith's most severe tests come not when we see nothing, but when we see a stunning array of evidence that seems to prove our faith in vain. —Elisabeth Elliot

We wonder why is God allowing this? That is when we have to trust God to shape us into a new form, bending us, without breaking us. We have to trust Him to know how much we can handle, and that

He won't give us more than that. At the time, it seems like what we are dealing with is already more than we can take.

I feel like we have been instructed by God to stand and take it. We have taken it. When does the victory come? How many more times will we be beaten down? Where is our rescuer? Haven't we turned to God for everything? Haven't we prayed before every decision? Where are you, God? Why haven't You rescued us? How much more, Lord? When does the victory come?

But we are still here and God is still good.

Job, the man in the Old Testament, knows how I feel. Our child was taken and then our air conditioning broke down, our computer died, I got very sick, our bills were crippling and then there was the smothering grief. We were ready to collapse.

Miraculously, God held us up each day. What the Bible says is true, "we are surrounded, but not destroyed. We are hard-pressed on every side, yet not crushed; we are perplexed, but not in despair" (2 Corinthians 4:8 NKJV).

Each thing seemed like it would be enough to break us, but we have been gifted by God with the ability to get up each morning and start fresh. We are lost and confused, but we will not curse God and die (Job 2:9).

One day we will see victory. Until then we breathe and carry on.

> Fear is the contradiction of faith. Faith says, "Whatever it is, it'll be okay because of God." —James MacDonald

Four facts can help you gain perspective during this time:
1. God is in control
2. God loves you
3. God sees the big picture
4. God knows the end

This struggle is personified in the movie, *The Drop Box*. Billed as the story of a pastor who rescues abandoned babies, the real story is how he and his wife raise their disabled son.

We follow them through those first few years of having a child whose disabilities leave them homeless, exhausted, desperate, and lost. One day they decide to use this event to change their outlook on life. They befriend other parents of disabled children, share their faith with the nurses and doctors in the hospital, adopt special-needs children, and end up making a drop box for abandoned babies.

They saved thousands of children.

Their church became a living organism of volunteers to care for these children twenty-four hours a day, and who will in turn care for the pastor's son long after the pastor and his wife pass away.

When news coverage inspired people in other countries to do the same thing, one family's struggle became a global movement. You can watch some of the movie at MarieWhiteAuthor.com. Click on the "Strength for Parents" tab and click the book link button.

This family's tragedy caused a thousand miracles, and yours can too.

Greg Laurie has said that non-Christians watch Christians during times of crisis, to see if we will fall. When you come through a crisis with your faith intact, you earn the right to speak out for Jesus. You earn the right to share your faith with others.

I think that the movie *X-Men* gets it right when Professor Xavier goes back in time, to convince his younger self to face his pain. His younger self says that the pain overwhelms him and the older Xavier says, "We need you to hope again." Watch the clip at www.MarieWhiteAuthor.com and click on the "Strength for Parents" tab.

> Man can live about forty days without food, about three days without water, about eight minutes without air ... but only for one second without hope. —Hal Lindsey

Chuck Swindoll said, "God has given us a purpose for our existence, a reason to go on, even though that existence includes tough times. Living through suffering we become sanctified—in other words, set apart for the glory of God. We gain perspective. We grow deeper. We grow up."

> Those who leave everything in God's hand, will eventually see God's hand in everything. —Unknown

If your life was a movie, would this be the point when everything has gone wrong and the main characters lose hope? The audience watches the movie and they want to yell at the screen for you to keep going because victory is right around the corner, but you are about to lose faith.

When I am the only one who has hope that our child will return I remind myself that others want our child to come home, they just haven't opened themselves up to hope. As James MacDonald said, "Hope is not the default position. It takes work to hope. Negativity is easy and natural."

The Bible says that faith means believing in something that can't be seen. "Now faith is confidence in what we hope for and assurance about what we do not see." (Hebrews 11:1 NIV)

We've read about people who have overcome life's crushing events to impact lives for thousands of years. They have lived like Malcolm Muggeridge who said, "I look back on experiences that at the time seemed especially desolating and painful with particular satisfaction. Indeed ... everything that has truly enhanced and enlightened my existence has been through affliction and not through happiness."

Throughout this book I have tried not to over-promise and under-deliver. You wanted someone who has been through the unimaginable to tell you that you will survive your own struggles. You will. You hoped that we would share some of the same feelings. We do. You wanted a new way to think about what you are passionate about and what your purpose may be. You have one.

I wanted to give you some simple, achievable goals such as the weekly checklists to improve your mind and body. I hoped that letting you see my pain would bond us through the thoughts and feelings you and I share. It's been my privilege to walk this road with you. Let me encourage you to keep a journal or write your story, since many people find it healing for them. When I wrote *Strength for Parents of Missing Children,* one parent said, "I really admire and appreciate what you're doing. So many of us can't find the words."

As I said at the beginning, it's a terrible privilege to write from pain.

Don't waste this time that God has appointed for you. If you haven't realized it yet, the time is a gift. *Most people will live without ever taking the opportunity to evaluate what makes life worth living.* They also won't notice that years have passed, and they have accomplished nothing. You know how precious time is and you know that you can never get it back. Endeavor to use every moment of your life to do, to be, and find the good. Every day, attack the enemy with prayer.

Pray:
- Lord, make me willing, to be made willing.
- Help me be a light in the darkness.
- Give me faith in Your ability to turn struggles into something wonderful.
- Let my faith point others to You.
- Make my struggle worth something bigger.
- Send ministering angels to comfort me (Hebrews 1:14.)
- Soften the hearts of those who fight against me.
- Make me bold, fearless and impactful.
- Give me strength and hope.
- Teach me how to have joy in You.
- Tell me who to pray for.
- God, Your will be done.

Colossians 3:15 says, "Let the peace of Christ rule in your hearts, since as members of one body you were called to peace. And be thankful."

He says to "let" the peace rule. It's a choice that we make. We have to let God give us peace, and give thanks for whatever good we have.

Dance, even when you don't feel like it. Turn up the music until you can't hear your heartbreak, and dance like your life depends on it; maybe it does.

In the moments when it feels like God can't be trusted, God doesn't keep His promises, God doesn't care, God doesn't save, God doesn't defeat, good doesn't have victory over evil, God doesn't hear, hope is lost and your side is not stronger, remember that God never abandons His own.

If you want to know the end of my story, visit me at my website www.MarieWhiteAuthor.com and tell me yours.

Like Joseph and Esther, you and I have been guests on the reality show, *Flip this Life- Extreme Makeover Edition*. God buys us "as is" and transforms us into something amazing. He does this by leading us through hardship and on to victory.

Victory comes to those who persevere.

And we will persevere.

Don't give up. Your victory could be right around the corner.

What crossing the finish line looks like is up to God, just play your part. Will you let God use you?

It's your turn to choose how your story will end.

When you face hard times, are afraid, or want to quit, gather just enough courage to face the next battle. You don't have to face all of them at once. "Therefore do not worry about tomorrow, for tomorrow will worry about itself. Each day has enough trouble of its own." (Matthew 6:24)

Even if the worst happens, you can emerge a changed person, transforming from caterpillar to butterfly. Or, you can stay in the cocoon of despair.

The choice is yours.

As for me and my house, we will choose to trust in the Lord.

> Therefore we do not lose heart. Though outwardly we are wasting away, yet inwardly we are being renewed day by day. For our light and momentary troubles are achieving for us an eternal glory that far outweighs them all. So we fix our eyes not on what is seen, but on what is unseen, since what is seen is temporary, but what is unseen is eternal. —2 Corinthians 4:16-18

And we know that in all things God works for the good of those who love him, who have been called according to his purpose (Romans 8:28).

II

Part Two

CHAPTER 14

Hearing from Others

This chapter is an excerpt of the interviews from
Strength for Parents of Missing Children.
They are included to inspire you.

Logan Clarke

An interview with Logan Clarke, internationally renowned private investigator and locator of missing children.

MARIE- Mr. Clarke, thank you for speaking with me today. You are the go-to guy for missing children and have been doing this for 30 years. How did you get that reputation?

LOGAN- My job was an in-country asset during the Vietnam War. Basically, we would rescue people. When I came back to the states I started doing the same thing, rescues, kidnap rescues, hostage negotiations, that sort of thing. It was just a natural rollover into rescuing children. I rescued girls from human trafficking when I was in southeast Asia. When I came here in the late 70s or early 80s, I tried to tell people that human trafficking was coming and they called me "Chicken Little." They said that only happens in third-world countries. I said, "You're out of your mind." And now it's on every single TV channel.

MARIE- It's amazing that you saw that coming. What is the first thing you tell a parent who hires you?

LOGAN- I'll be the a**. You be the poor father or mother who wants their children back, I'll be the one who gets mad and calls everyone a**holes and yells that they're not doing their job. Everyone can get mad at me, that's what I'm here for. Everyone needs to look at you and know that you're the nicest person, who only wants their children back and you're the victim.

MARIE- That's good advice. It's hard not to go into fierce, protective mode when your children are being harmed. But you're right, fear often comes out as anger, and that makes parents look unstable or worse yet, guilty. What do you feel like families are least prepared for?

LOGAN- It's a rollercoaster they're on. But they need to listen to me. I say, do exactly what I tell you. If I tell you I want something— get it for me, and if you can't get it for me, let me know and I'll get it. And don't lie to me. If you lie to me and I find out you lied to me, I will turn it right back on you. If you did something wrong and you lie to me, I'll throw your a** in jail. Then I'll use your money, that you paid me, to investigate you. The first thing I'm gonna do is investigate you, with your money. I've got to be convinced that you're telling the truth, the absolute truth. I can't gamble. If you say there's never been domestic violence, you think I'm just gonna believe you? Not on your life. Nor would the cops. And they wouldn't respect me if I just took your word for it.

God forbid you beat your wife up and here I am being your champion, and that's why she ran away.

MARIE- What would you tell a parent who has just experienced parental abduction?

LOGAN- Stay calm, don't do anything stupid.

And I tell 'em don't expect this to end fast. And I rarely, rarely, ever promise a parent I'll get their children back, unless I have that gut feeling. Unless I look at the facts and I know in my gut. I said it to Steven in Texas, and when I found out the kids were in Mexico, in the cartel area, I regretted promising. I went, "Damn, why did I do that?" I got 'em though.

MARIE- Bret and I have become friends through this. How did Bret find out about you?

LOGAN- Bret read the article about Steven James' boys and found him, they talked for a couple of days and then Bret talked to me.

MARIE- What have you seen when children come home?

LOGAN- They are extremely confused. The majority of times they have been told terrible things about the other parent. The alienation starts right away. In very rare cases the parent will say, "I don't want to say anything bad about your mother or father."

MARIE- What is it like when you go to get the child?

LOGAN- It's most dangerous between the rescue and getting them to the parent. This is the most dangerous time. In the rare case when we can't take a parent with us to get the child, I take a piece of clothing with the parent's smell on it. The best thing is the kid's blanket. We put it to the child's face, they smell that familiar smell and you can instantly feel their heart rate goes down. Then we put on a video or Skype of the parent saying, "Hi honey it's mommy and this is my friend Logan, he's going to bring you home to me." All of that is happening in the back of a van, while we're speeding down the street.

MARIE- How has this job affected your family life?

LOGAN- One day I was at Walmart with my daughter and I have a very distinctive voice, people remember it for years. As I was talking to my little girl I hear a man behind me say, "Excuse me sir, are you Logan Clarke?"

I never know what to expect. I've had people say, "Logan Clarke," and it's a guy I've put away for five years, "I've been waiting five years for this." And they pull a knife and jump me.

But I said, "Yes."

I turned around to look at this guy and he has a seven-year-old boy with him and the guy says, "Bobby, you need to hug this man."

Bobby looked at his dad and then at me, and his dad said, "Remember when you were kidnapped and you were taken away? This is the man who brought you home to me." And this kid ran to me and hugged me. People were applauding, tears were rolling down their faces. At that moment my daughter realized that even though it was sad to have me gone a lot, I was doing something greater and more important than being home all the time.

MARIE- Besides reuniting families, what other satisfaction do you find in this line of work?

LOGAN- The greatest thing that my clients tell me— the first night after they hire me— 9 times out of 10, is that, "Last night was the first night I've slept since this happened. I'm so relieved. Not that you've promised me anything, but I know that I have someone who cares. I know there's someone who really knows what they are doing, who is on my side, who is helping me. And for the first time, I could actually get rest."

That's a great reward.

That's what I want them to feel.

I don't want them to get overconfident. I always caution them that I'm not going to come busting in their door with an S across my chest and their children in a jar. It's going to take time and money and a lot of patience. There will be ups and downs. The only thing I can guarantee is change. Change is the only constant and it changes hourly and daily.

I also do a lot of other kinds of cases like elder abuse, con men, hidden asset work, stalkers, you name it. I handled the Casey Kasem case, where his wife kidnapped him from the hospice facility he was at. But I can't do undercover work anymore because I'm too recognizable.

MARIE- What do you hope will happen to help missing children?

LOGAN- I have often said that it will take some high-powered senator to have their child kidnapped by the other parent before they will do something about it. Then we'll hear about it in congress. Then they'll say, "This is absurd. We've got to do something about this and I know just the man to tell you about it. I'd like to introduce you to Mr. Logan Clarke." That's what it takes. An important legislator has to go through this before there will be action.

MARIE- The cases you take have made you world famous. Has that helped you get authorities to act?

LOGAN- I've begged district attorneys to debate me on TV. No one will do it because they will get slammed.

There were two boys kidnapped from Texas, it took me six months to find out they were in Mexico. In the deepest part of Mexico, cartel area, took me five months to figure out how to get them out. I sent special operations guys in and they told me that it would be a bloodbath. They came back, said we couldn't do it that way. I went to NBC and said, "Follow me on this case and it will be some of the best stuff you've ever done." They followed me for four and a half months. I mean, we did everything and we got those kids back. It took 11 months. And NBC? They were given the Edward R. Murrow award for that kidnapping coverage.

MARIE- What reception do you get from law enforcement?

LOGAN- I've been with Texas Rangers who tell me that the kids aren't in any danger because they're with the mother, and I tell them, "Oh, really? Do you know that the mother is on psychotic meds? And she's not taking them because I'm tracking her through her medications and the minute she fills her prescription she's going to be caught and she knows that. So guess what? She's not taking her meds. And she's bipolar."

Two weeks after that conversation a different mother stabbed her child, right after she kidnapped them from the father. Stabbed and killed. None of it makes sense. They aren't a good mommy or a good daddy. They are kidnappers.

What I'm saying can be factually backed up and facts are facts. When you assume a child is okay because the mother kidnapped them, you are putting them in jeopardy. But the Department of Justice is quoted as saying that parental kidnapping is extreme child abuse.

MARIE- Do you ever plan to stop doing this line of work?

LOGAN- I went to the doctor and they said that if I didn't get out of this career, I would die. Not of a bullet, but of a heart attack. They said that my stress levels were off the chart, even higher than someone who had just come back from Vietnam.

MARIE- If you decide to retire where are these families going to go?

LOGAN- I have a team. I have other people who will hopefully take over. I still like to save people. It gets in your blood. I'd still like to do one difficult case a year.

MARIE- You've talked about retiring. What do you want people to know that you stood for?

LOGAN- That I fought for the people who couldn't fight for themselves.

I grew up without my dad and something that affected me all my life was that my dad would show up every couple of years and take us to back-to-school shopping. I was about 8 and my brother was about 10 and we were parked in an alley. We were walking into a store when a woman started screaming. This guy was running, a little guy about 5'7", down the alley with a purse. Right behind him was this old woman saying, "Stop him. He stole my purse. Stop him."

My dad was a fireman, 6'2", he'd been a marine on the islands, and I'm thinking, "Cool, my dad is going to stop this guy and get the purse and help this lady."

My dad drops his hands and pushes my brother and I back, and the guy runs right in front of him. He could have put his leg out and tripped the guy. He'd been a marine! But he did nothing. The guy runs right by us. The woman runs up and looks at my dad, sweat pouring down off her forehead and said, "You couldn't even trip him?" And she just walked off.

I said, "Dad, why didn't you—" And he said, "Don't get involved in other people's problems."

From that day on I knew that I was going to get involved in other people's problems. I lost all respect for him and I never forgot it. It still bothers me. This was in the fifties. The guy didn't have a gun. I could have tripped him. It was devastating.

That's what motivated me.

If I'm at a club and some guy is beating up his wife, I'm the first one who's going to be at that table and I'm gonna knock that guy out. I don't care who he is. I'm going to grab him off that table and have him arrested.

MARIE- I see that your website talks about a film being made about you. Are you allowed to tell me about it?

LOGAN- They guys who wrote *The Fighter* and *Patriots Day*, both starring Mark Wahlberg, have been working for a year on a script about my life.

I give them lots of material. It seems like I have a habit of getting myself into some pretty crazy situations.

I'll go after a child and I'll wind up in the middle of a third world narcotics ring that the uncle of the kid I'm after runs. You know, he runs the cartel, and the least of my problems is getting the kid, because they think I'm there to arrest them and take all their drugs. All I want is the kid.

I've had that happen many times. So, it's not necessarily just who you're going after, but who all the relatives are.

I went after a child in Brazil and the father-in-law was a colonel in the Brazilian army. My client was almost killed.

They wrapped him in duct tape, put him in the back of a car, and had a gun to him. They were taking him out to the woods to shoot him in the head. A roadblock they didn't expect happened to be there looking for rebels. They looked in the backseat and saw this guy huddled down with duct tape around him and a shootout broke out. They killed the two guys and my client was freed.

We've had some insane things happen.

MARIE- How do you cope with what you've seen?

LOGAN- I believe very much in what I'm doing. I'd like parents to know that I'm not as hard and cold as I look and sound. There is a whole other side to me.

They can get my books on Amazon or Barnes and Noble. I have a book called *Just Passing Through* that Hallmark published: http://a.co/fqHV20n and another one called, Last Night an Angel Stopped By: http://a.co/66O6INC that's a true story of when I was in intensive care and a woman died.

I wrote *The Legend of the Teardrop Tree* for my clients. I know what sadness is and what they've been through. It's about a tree that is sort of a cross between a weeping willow and a banyan tree, that has little teardrops coming down the leaves. The tree says, "Let your sorrow fall on me. I'll cry for you. I'm the teardrop tree."

The animator from *The Lion King* did the illustrations.

It's for kids and it's about how to deal with pain and sorrow and loss. It's the kind of book a parent reads to their child: http://a.co/amrAvy1

That keeps me sane. What I've seen and been involved with in the world makes you very, very, very calloused. It changes you. If you look at those books and you look at me, then look at my background, you'd say, "Impossible, this guy didn't write these books." It's just a whole different side.

I never go to a counselor and that's because of my writing. Writing keeps me sane. Right now I'm working on my memoir.

MARIE- You've left such a legacy. I am privileged to be able to talk with you and share your knowledge with others. Thank you for all that you do.

Dr. Sue Cornbluth

Dr. Cornbluth specializes in high conflict divorce, and is a nationally recognized parenting expert.

MARIE- Dr. Sue Cornbluth, as an expert in family reunification, what would you like parents to know?

DR. SUE- I would like them to remember that their children have a relationship history with them. Kids don't forget that. Alienated kids may be afraid to tell you because they are afraid of their alienator. But parents should never give up on their children. Their children do not want them to give up, even when the children are pushing them away. These kids are just manipulated and they don't know what to do. When they are cursing you out, telling you to go away and that they hate you, they are expressing the pain that they are experiencing from their alienator. But they **need** you. Don't ever quit.

Another thing I would tell parents is that patience is your virtue. Even if a judge orders reunification therapy and the other parent doesn't do it, that judge isn't going to hold them in contempt of court, because it's only a recommendation. Family court is not designed to reunify you with your child. It just isn't. I want to be clear on that. It's designed to decide two things usually, custody and child support.

I don't know how the country got the idea that family court is there to reunify you with your children. They're not. That's why there are people out there like me, doing this, and that's your best approach.

MARIE- What does it look like when children come home?

DR. SUE- When a child comes home you must go slow and you must earn back their trust. It's not like they come home and everything is peachy. It's not.

Never push these kids to talk. They don't trust easily, they will be watching you like a hawk and they are going to be angry. They are going to say, "Why did you let me go? I don't want to be here with you. You are horrible." You have to expect that. You have to be accepting, validating, and acknowledge that they have experienced pain over this. In time things can get better.

MARIE- You're saying that when children come home, actions will speak louder than words?

DR. SUE- That is exactly right, your kids are always watching you, seeing if you will mess up, just like their alienator is saying you will. You have to be in a strong place to do the work of getting your children back. And sometimes people are not in the place to do that. It doesn't mean that you don't break down sometimes, you're only human. But most people report that they have become stronger themselves from the work they do with me.
 I tell them that I'm sorry you are being watched all the time, but show through your actions that you are not who the alienator is making you out to be. Don't do it through your words, but through your actions.

MARIE- What do you tell a parent who has limited contact with their child?

DR. SUE- I tell parents to stop telling their kids over and over that you love them and that you miss them. Because in your kid's mind, if you love them and miss them, then why aren't you with them? The kids wonder why they are with the bad parent? The kids are thinking, "If you love me and miss me, why are you so mean to me?"
 And that's what they're being told by the alienator.
 It's normal to tell your children that you love them and miss them, but they already know that.

What your kids are looking for is for you to confirm their truth. Their truth is that you have abandoned them. Even though it may not be your truth.

MARIE- We never think that a child would be looking for the "good" parent to mess up. It sounds like in alienation, kids can be hurt and manipulated to the point that they are looking for a way to validate what they have been told. How did you figure this out?

DR. SUE- I started out in foster care, working with children who had been abused. I also worked with the adoptive parents. Kids who had been abused had self-esteem issues because they would define themselves by what they had been through or told by their birth parents.

I left foster care and taught for years as a professor of psychology at Temple University. I was there with my doctorate in clinical psychology, sitting in my graduate program and thinking, "This may not be for me."

I like to educate, give tools, strategize, and take action. That's how I got involved with parent alienation. I was interested in a case where I couldn't understand why the parents could not separate themselves from the fight and put their child first.

So I read the materials available on parent alienation by all the experts. All of these books were saying, this is how it happens, but nobody was doing anything to change it.

As I researched it I realized that there was no one to give parents any guidance, skills or tools. The alienated parents were scared and didn't know what to do and the kids were being harmed by this.

So I decided to do something that no one else was doing. I would take the next step and design action plans to help alienated families.

Then I found this person that many people don't know about, Jane Major. She did a lot of work in parental alienation and never got credit. Jane understood exactly what was going on and she had a course called *Breakthrough Parenting*. Half the course was on parent

Alienation, which no one else was offering. So I took the course and was certified to do parent alienation coaching.

MARIE- I'm sure you're unique in your qualifications to help parents as both a Doctor of Psychology and certified in parent alienation. How do you work with clients?

DR. SUE- I'm very hands-on, even though I have clients from England to India. Anyone who doesn't live close to me communicates on Skype or by phone. Parental alienation is becoming a world-wide phenomenon and an epidemic that people are not paying attention to.

One of the things that comes out again and again is that the parent who is keeping the other parent away is very narcissistic, they care more about themselves than their children. One of the areas I focused on in my doctoral training was personality disorders. Narcissistic personality disorder is identified in the DSM-V. And what does the narcissist want? They want to be told that they are right. They want their ego stroked.

What I'm saying is that there are ways to get into a narcissist's mind and make change. I've done it in hundreds of cases. It may not be the relationship you've dreamed of with your alienated child, but it will be better than what you had before. Because many parents have nothing.

MARIE- Do you ever have to turn parents away?

DR. SUE- A lot of times people call me too late and say, "I wish I would have found out about you five years ago." Not every case can be solved. Not every case can be helped.

There are certain factors that I look for to help reunite an alienated parent with their child. Two of those factors are:

1. Do you have contact with your ex in any way?
2. Do you have contact with your children?

If there is a restraining order against you, and you can't have any contact with your children, then I can't help you. There's no way for me to be able to get you in contact with your ex.

MARIE- What's so different about working with you?

DR. SUE- People will call me and say, "You won't be able to help me. No one's been able to help me."

And I say, "That's because you have probably seen a therapist who has not been trained in parental alienation." Parental alienation was never taught to me as a therapist.

Traditional therapy doesn't work in these situations. You need strategies, you need tools, you need specific language to break through to your children, and to your ex. That's what I teach people.

The difference is that when you work with me, you have an action plan tailored to your case, because every case is different. And this is not therapy where we just talk to you once a week. We are working with you on this every day. It has to be done like that.

MARIE- I love your fresh attitude and go-to personality. It really comes across in your videos. You seem like an action taker.

DR. SUE- Correct. And people love that.

I have not been through parental alienation myself, and I can't imagine not being with my kids, even for a day. Because of that, I do this work. I don't want parents to feel that pain. I don't want children to feel that pain. That's why I do it, because it is unfair to the children.

MARIE- How can parents work with you?

DR. SUE- I have a website, DrSueAndYou.com where they can get a free 30 minute consultation. There are also videos on the website and I have a blog.

Not everyone can afford private coaching, so I have a new online classroom coming out. That way I can help as many people as possible.

An online course was one of the things a lot of parents contacted me about.

Before I accept anyone as a client, I have them send me some texts or emails between them and the alienator or children. What target parents think is a harmless text to the alienator, usually isn't. They can't see it because the target parents aren't objective, they've been hurt.

I recommend that when you are communicating with your ex don't use the word "you" as in, "You did this or you did that." It doesn't work. Pointing fingers causes blame, not coming together.

MARIE- How do you deal with this on a daily basis and still manage to be there for your family? How do you find balance?

DR. SUE- I've had to learn over the years you have to balance your time. Take time and be nurturing to yourself. I don't always do it, but I have become better at that over the years. Nothing in this world matters to me more than my children and making sure that they are stable and balanced. I also have a wonderful and supportive husband.

There are days when I'm off balance. I don't believe in perfection. We all make mistakes.

MARIE- Tell me about your book.

DR. SUE- My book came out in 2014 and I wanted to call it *Building Self-Esteem in Kids That Were Traumatized*. It came out at the time of the Sandy Hook school shooting. But the publisher came up with a different title, *Building Self-Esteem in Children and Teens Who Are Adopted or Fostered*. The book can be used for any child who has gone through trauma.

A lot of my clients have bought it and said that it really helped them learn how to reconnect with their alienated children. Alienation is abuse.

MARIE- Dr. Cornbluth, I am so thankful for your time and for providing this strategic guidance for all of the parents with missing children. Thank you.

To find out more about Dr. Cornbluth's book and services visit www.DrSueandYou.com.

Dr. Raymond Mitsch

Dr. Mitsch is the chair of the Psychology Department at Colorado Christian University and is the best-selling author of *Grieving the Loss of Someone You Love.*

MARIE- Dr. Mitsch, as an expert in grief, can you explain what is happening to the bodies of parents with missing children?

DR. MITSCH- One of the problems is the ongoing hyper-vigilance of waiting for more news. Psychologically that puts parents in a state where their bodies are cranking out a lot of cortisol. Because we can only stay vigilant for a certain period of time, the body seems to cycle, and then it wanes. With that waning there is a quiet period. Something as simple as news coming in or a phone call, can trigger the cortisol and adrenaline, then you're back to vigilance again.

I think the cycle is oftentimes what takes the greatest toll on parents. The reality is when someone loses someone to death or the end of a relationship, there is what I call a period to the end of the sentence. There is an end. In the case of a missing, runaway child, or even prodigal child, you don't have a period (.) anymore, you have the three dots of an ellipses (...).

Which means that it's a continuation. I think that weighs heavily on a lot of parents' bodies as they wait for news that their child is going to return.

I would suggest that parents be around a group of people who can support them by being vigilant for them. This way they can get some rest, because they know that someone is tracking the information that is coming in.

People experiencing a missing child experience a deterioration in their bodily systems. The reality is that all of us have certain systems that are more reactive to stress than others. For some people it's felt in their intestinal tract, others experience symptoms in their cardiovascular system. Each person will have a unique presentation of stress with a child that is missing.

MARIE- What are some behaviors that we should expect to see as we experience grief and loss?

DR. MITSCH- You're describing three layers of trauma. There's the grief that their child is gone, the fear of what the child may be experiencing and the pain that the parent is not there to help them. That's a multi-layered kind of grief. Where the parent is emotionally during a specific time of the day, will probably determine what layer they're in.

There is a wide gamut of ways I see people experience grief, it ranges from physiological (bodily) responses to behavioral responses.

Most of our efforts, when it comes to grieving, are really directed toward containing the pain.

Sometimes that's mummifying the room, like Queen Victoria is said to have done when her consort died. She even sent the butler to his room each morning with the shaving kit and had it brought back at night.

This is really a way of trying to minimize the impact of the reality of what's been lost. In the beginning, that is pretty normal. It's part of denial and trying to manage how we accept the reality of what has happened.

The other thing I see are behaviors that express psychological things. Depression, sadness, fatigue, poor appetite or increased sleeping, tends to misdiagnose people who are grieving as depressed. Alternately, there are anxiety symptoms such as restlessness, poor sleep, panic attacks, anxiety, unusual reactions to things or phantom experiences and these are also natural.

My dad died when I was a kid and I had phantom experiences. You could almost set the clock by when my dad came home from the steel mill and I would still hear the back door open.

All of those behaviors are us trying to absorb a reality that we fundamentally reject. Everybody has a different way to do that. In the grief response I see a lot of opposites. People either spending too much time going over what is going on or has happened, or the other alternative is packing everything up, putting their stuff away, and pretending the person was never there.

I've seen a lot of people do that. They erase all trace of the person because the reminders are so painful.

Usually, in that situation, I will tell people to box things up and put them away, but don't get rid of things. At a later time, when they are ready, they can get the box out and decide what to keep.

Someone spending a lot of time ruminating on the person who is absent, experiencing the "if onlys" or "should haves" is really trying to change their reality.

"If only I had spent more time with them." Or, "If only I had made sure that they went to the doctor."

Then there are the "should haves" where we make demands of ourselves with information we didn't have. The "should haves" always come after the fact.

Generally people's reactions fall within the broad range of what we would call "normal behaviors." However, some can go to the outer edges where the person becomes suicidal. Then we need to be more careful and make referrals to a mental health professional for evaluation.

MARIE- As Christians, what is different about grief for you and I?

DR. MITSCH- One of the myths that people have is that if you're a Christian you either don't or shouldn't grieve. I couldn't disagree more.

In 1 Thessalonians, Paul talks about how he doesn't want the believers to grieve like those who have no hope and that's probably the core of the answer. Here Paul implies that we *will* grieve and experience all the symptoms of grieving.

Whether that's the result of trying to grasp what has happened or as an expression of the emotions from the absence of the person, a Christian will still experience those same feelings. The difference is that we know the nature of God's heart and His love for us. He loved us enough to send His son to die for us.

It also means that our grief is not going to waste.

You are going to grieve. Parents will experience the absence of their children and the hole that is left behind.

In psychology, we use the T.E.A.R. model:
-To accept the loss of the person
-Experience the emotions that go with it
-Adjust to life without the person &
-Reinvest in life again

A lot of people still refer to the stages of grief, but the problem with stages is that they are just too linear. People generally experience grief in waves or cycles and I think that Christians do too. Our faith does not preclude the grief that we experience.

The hope you have is not in what is happening to your child, but the hope we have is in God and His love for us. We know there's a lot more happening in the situation than meets the eye.

MARIE- What advice would you give to parents who have lost their identity?

DR. MITSCH- There are two issues at hand, one is the fear of what the children are going through and the other is the loss of the parent's purpose or identity. Parents pride themselves, in some sense, on the level of power they have in protecting their kids. When kids are lost or taken, it blows that concept away and adds another level of loss.

Who am I now, without this child?

What kind of parent am I, because I wasn't able to protect them?

The impact on the parent largely depends on the age at which the child is removed. It's safe to say that the younger the child, the more complicated the grief.

The reality is that it's easier to define ourselves with tangible objects. When I say I'm a parent, usually I give proof to that fact with my children.

What people tend to say is that you're still a parent, even though your child is not around. But that doesn't really address the heart-level issue. We inevitably define ourselves by the people around us because we're firmly grounded in relationships.

Recognize that you have lost more than your child and that there is a grief process to readjusting to a new identity. This is especially difficult for people taking care of young children or elderly parents, because your lives get centered around the tasks that you do for them. You have to adjust to a new environment without the tasks of taking care of the missing child. When those tasks are taken away, we feel very lost.

MARIE- You're right! It's almost like going down steps with a hand-rail and then suddenly the railing is gone and you sort of lose your balance. It takes a few seconds to regain your balance and get a sense of where your body is in relationship to the stairs.

DR. MITSCH- You have to recalibrate to a different environment that doesn't have that child in it. You have to figure out what to do now and begin to structure your emotional relationships and the physical tasks you do around a new normal.

MARIE- You are also an author, what are your books about?

DR. MITSCH- I have written five books, but I think there are two that might interest your readers. The first is *Grieving the Loss of Someone You Love* and the other is *Nurturing Your Child's Potential*.

MARIE- Those sound terrific. Dr. Mitsch, your insights into grief are really impressive. There are so many aspects that most of us have never thought of and you have been able to walk us through them. I really appreciate your time. Thank you.

Dr. Mitsch is the Associate Professor and chair of the Psychology Department at Colorado Christian University. His books are available on Amazon and you can read his blog at www.drmitsch.com.

Dr. Timothy Benson

Dr. Benson is a Lecturer in Psychiatry at Harvard Medical School and founded a company that provides strategic support for high-performers and their families.

MARIE- Dr. Benson, as a psychiatrist who works with people in high-stress environments, such as NFL players, have you worked with anyone going through a painful divorce?

DR. BENSON- I have. Professional athletes must perform in high-stress conditions that not only take a toll on them personally, but also on their family life. This is likely the reason behind the reports that the divorce rate of athletes can range from 60 to 80%.

When an athlete goes through something like a divorce there can be an overwhelming sense of guilt and remorse, as they struggle to find meaning or redefine themselves in their current situation.

Out of a multitude of questions, the biggest question becomes, "What now?"

As they grieve they are also forced to grapple with how to effectively deal with this loss, while attempting to prepare for the unknown.

MARIE- That is very similar to what parents of missing children experience. What have you found to help people manage the identity crisis of a major life-change?

DR. BENSON- When there is a monumental change in your life it can be very destabilizing. Big changes also can illicit major loses including: the loss of identity, the loss of structure, and in some cases the loss of purpose. All of these changes can cause an emotional upheaval.

To this end, I often suggest three key strategies to help deal with what I call, "traumatic" changes.

Stay **grounded**. You need to get grounded in things like your values, your mission, your drive or your hope. Once you determine what those are, then you start to organize around them.

A big change in your circumstances can expose a faulty foundation, it also presents the opportunity to rebuild on a new one.

Part of being grounded is confronting uncomfortable truths. Where people get into trouble is when they cling to what *was*, instead of embracing what *is*.

2. Develop and operate out of a sense of **gratitude**. Gratitude, while sounding touchy-feely, is really grounding. Sometimes it's gratitude for the journey, other times it's gratitude for the things that you have overcome. Either way, you also need to express gratitude for those people how have helped you thus far. Successful people must connect with others and find a higher purpose.

It's important to look at things in a different, more productive light.

3. Maintain a **growth mindset**. You almost need to think like a beginner. A lot of times people handle things in a certain way and are successful. Then, when they have a disruption and are destabilized, they are too rigid and won't change. That prohibits personal growth. Whereas the person who is open to growing, may see new possibilities in their life.

Having a positive mindset is paramount.

MARIE- Parents of missing children define success as being reunited with their child. When reunification happens, in addition to their joy, there will be issues. What can they expect?

DR. BENSON- George Bernard Shaw was quoted in saying, "There are but two tragedies in life. One is to lose your heart's desire. The other is to gain it." What this is saying is that as good as things can be you must also be prepared for unexpected challenges and unintended consequences. There is going to be a transition time and it's not going to be perfect. One thing to watch for, when a child comes back into the household, is the potential pull of perpetually overcompensating for the loss. This could lead to enabling behaviors, since guilt or fear might drive you to be more lenient than you would normally be. Be careful not to over-compensate to the point that it becomes detrimental to the positive aspects of reunification. The key would be to allow an adjustment period, but don't stray too far away from your true values.

Another caution I would give is to be careful of what you're organizing around. You will never forget and you don't need to pass over what has happened, but developing or finding a new healthy reference point to rally around will be important. This is where gratitude can play a major role.

MARIE- That is great advice. Reading your book, I became aware that even in success there are losses. What are some losses you've seen successful people face?

DR. BENSON- In my book I focus on the challenges of people who work in high-stress environments and I help them deal with the consequences of success. One of those losses they face is the loss of community. Some family members and friends will hold success against them. They will say, "Now that you're making money, you think that you're better than us." The reality is that the demands and expectations of the culture of high competition differ from those of the family of origin. Failing to reconcile those differences and the emotions they illicit can lead to the loss of important connections in your life.

MARIE- I could see that happening to those who are active in the parental alienation or grief communities. Once they are reunited they either drop out of the groups, because they don't need them anymore, or they leave because hurting members of the group act out from jealousy.

Thank you for making time in your busy schedule to talk to me about this. I know that many things you shared will strike a chord with readers.

You can read about the seven skills to handling success in Dr. Benson's book *Surviving Success*, available at http://a.co/brq1O0z.

Dr. Timothy Gerard Benson is a Lecturer in Psychiatry at Harvard Medical School and founder of the Benson Performance Group, a company that provides strategic support for high-performers and their families at www.DrTimothyBenson.com.

Michael Jeffries

Mr. Jeffries is a formerly alienated parent, a university speechwriter, and author of *A Family's Heartbreak*.

MARIE- Mike, let's dive right in. As a former alienated parent, what insights do you have for parents living through a missing child?

MICHAEL- The concept that time heals all wounds isn't really true. These are wounds that don't really heal, but time does deaden the sensation a little bit.

The searing pain I felt during the first few years turned into a manageable ache. It's almost like having a slightly sprained ankle, the pain doesn't stop you from walking and getting around, but you feel of it every time you take a step. Obviously, that's a more manageable place than getting caught up in the rollercoaster of intense emotions that overtake your life when alienation is fresh.

I also think that not forgetting the other people in your life is very important. If you have other children who are alienated, brothers, sisters, parents and friends, it's not fair to them that you are sitting right in front of them, but in essence they have lost you too.

Focusing on the people who are still there, making sure that you're still a good father or mother to the children who aren't alienated is important. Make sure you're still the good son or daughter to your parents. Make sure you're still a good friend. Focus on the people in front of you, instead of the one who's not.

The same thing goes with work. A lot of people get lost in their work when they suffer any type of loss, because work is a wonderful coping mechanism. It prevents us from thinking about that which is most painful. While I don't advocate that anyone become a workaholic, the people at work also deserve the person that you were before the alienation.

You can only expect so much out of your colleagues before you may have other issues, if you're not giving them what you were giving before the alienation. That's not to say that people at work aren't sympathetic. Believe me, they will give you plenty of time and plenty of space. I remember my boss coming to me during literally the worst day and saying, "We need you to focus for the next six hours. Can you focus for me for the next six hours?" I gave her that six hours. Then I went back to my office and started crying all over again. But I gave her my full effort for that six hours.

MARIE- What tips do you have about communicating with your alienated child?

MICHAEL- I think it's important to continue reaching out to the alienated child with those unconditional messages of love and forgiveness, but I did learn, that you don't do it on a really bad day. The day when you get a $500 car repair bill and someone has made your work day a nightmare, is not a good day to reach out to the alienated child to get rejected. It just makes things worse. The days to reach out are the days when you're having a really good day. Then the rejection doesn't bother you as much.

The best trick that I discovered was that when you're having a really bad day— go to bed. My philosophy was that things are always better in the morning. In the morning the slate is wiped clean from the day before. It's a new day with a new start and wonderful things can happen. Everything always looks better in the morning.

MARIE- How were you able to cope with the alienation?

MICHAEL- I think it's important to reach out to people who have walked in your shoes, but it's also important to keep your parental alienation in a box and only let it come out of the box a few times a day. Focusing on parental alienation can't be a 24/7 thing. Too much time on the parental alienation groups takes a toll on you; it increases your anger, increases the emotions and any negativity feeds off itself.

That's not a healthy place to hang out all the time. Remember there are things you enjoy like sports, reading, and hobbies. Get involved with people who are doing those things, so that your whole world doesn't become parental alienation and all the pain that is attached to it. Keep those outside interests, don't let them fall by the wayside.

I know it's hard. When you're going through this, the last thing you want to do is go to a book club or go to the gym, but you have to force yourself. That's how you cope.

MARIE- How were you able to get past the things that had been done to you and your child?

MICHAEL- I think that the biggest thing is letting go of the anger. This is huge and it's not something that people can get their arms around quickly. I discovered that anger is a wonderful coping mechanism. When you're angry you don't have to deal with much of anything. You can just stay angry. It's an outlet for you to deal with your emotions in a very negative way, and not deal with reality.

Until you can let go of the anger, you can never be the person that you were before the process started.

You really do have to forgive. That doesn't mean that you have to forget everything and set yourself up to be taken advantage of all over again. It can take a long time to learn to forgive, it took me years and years. But when I did, it became much easier to live with this burden.

I wouldn't have been able to write my book, if I was still angry. I would have come across as an angry, bitter person, griping about not getting what he wanted, and the book would have had no credibility.

But, because I had worked through the anger, the objectivity in the book really came through. So much of the positive feedback on the book, focused on its objectivity. I think that when you get over the anger, it allows you to look at your situation objectively, and maybe recognize where you could have done some things differently. You might even learn from the situation.

When you're angry you are diminishing the chances for you to reconnect with your child because when we're angry all that we want is to slam the other parent. We want validation. We want apologies. The alienated child isn't interested in giving you any of that. Your pain, your anger and your emotions are not even on the child's radar.

But once you get rid of the anger you can live in the present and future and focus on rebuilding your relationship with the child. The ability to stay out of the past and all the pain really helps the reunification process.

MARIE- Have you been reunified with your son?

MICHAEL- My son and I reconnected about five years ago, after a long twelve years. We have a great relationship. I wouldn't say that it's better than it would have been if we hadn't been alienated, because I don't think that would be true. But I couldn't ask for a better relationship with him. When we met for that first time, I kept the focus on him and his life. I showed him I was over the past and not angry at him or his mom. At one point, I purposely brought his mom up in a very generic, non-judgmental way. I saw him visibly tense when I mentioned her name, but when he saw it was just a casual reference to something we used to do as a family, he relaxed and enjoyed the conversation.

Now there's an openness between us that comes from the fact that he saw that there was no anger and that I was over it. That put him at ease, and allowed us to reconnect.

MARIE- Do you feel like you've grown and become a better version of yourself?

MICHAEL- Yes, I do believe I have. Part of it is perspective. Prior to being alienated, I would get worked up about things in life or at work, but now I realize that those aren't important. It's made me a calmer person and certainly more forgiving. If I can forgive the players in my story, then it's easy to forgive the guy who cuts me off in traffic or the co-worker who is a jerk. I'm also much more accepting than I used to be. My favorite expression is, "It is what it is."

MARIE- What is your profession?

MICHAEL- I am a speechwriter at a university.

MARIE- Then, writing your book *A Family's Heartbreak: A Parent's Introduction to Parental Alienation* wasn't much of a stretch for you.

MICHAEL- No, it wasn't. As I said in the introduction to the book, I've been a professional writer forever and I was keeping a journal, purely for the psychological and emotional benefits. Journaling is a good way to off-load emotions and deal with things. I began to realize that there might be something else going on when I started editing my copy, shortening sentences and changing verb tenses.
I began asking myself why I was making these changes and realized that the journal might help somebody else, someday. That's how the book came to be.

MARIE- Did you feel like there were times when anything someone said to you was going to be wrong?

MICHAEL- Yes. My wife couldn't win. No matter what she said about the situation, it was not going to make me happy. She deserves a medal for putting up with me and all those emotions during those years.
I think that people who have a really strong ego, those who know they're a good father/mother/professional/friend, can probably deal

with this better than those that don't have a strong ego. Because when people would come up to me and say, "He isn't ever coming back." I wouldn't fall apart, because I knew I was a good husband and father. Parental alienation wasn't my fault. It wasn't my kid's fault. I was doing all the things I need to do to ensure that he comes back one day. He may not come back according to my schedule, but one day he was going to come back.

The person who said, "He isn't coming back," didn't know what he was talking about.

Of course, when my wife would say, "It'll be OK, he'll come back." I had to say, "Yes, but not according to my timeframe." That's what I meant when I said she couldn't win.

I agreed that he was going to come home, but in the meantime I'm thinking, this still sucks.

One of the alienating parents' tactics is to make false accusations about you, there is always a time when you start to question your own sanity about things. You just can't believe that anyone would be crazy enough to make up the stuff you are accused of doing. That's when that strong sense of self really kicks in and you say, "Of course I didn't do that." The alienating parent is going to throw everything they can at you and see if something works.

With a strong sense of self or ego, you realize that you were a good parent, you are a good person and this is not a reflection of you as an individual.

I'll never forget that someone said to me, "I realize that this really sucks, but you've still got a roof over your head, you're not hungry, everybody's healthy and one day he'll come back. It may not be in the timeframe that you think it should, but just keep doing what you're doing and things will work out." As much as I didn't want to admit it at the time, that person was basically right.

MARIE- Were there things you found hard to handle during your alienation?

MICHAEL- TV, internet and radio are both your biggest enemy and your biggest helper. There's nothing worse than hearing a particular song on the radio and suddenly breaking down into tears. I would have to turn the station. It was the same with certain heartwarming scenes on TV. However, watching the news and seeing kids struggling with cancer, or dying from violence, really puts things into perspective. I realized that I didn't have it that bad.

Sometimes you have to take time to watch the shows on children in the cancer wards, because it helps you to remember that while you may not be able to see your child, at least he's healthy. He doesn't have IVs sticking out of his arms. If someone would have asked you before all of this, "Would you rather your kid be healthy and not in your life, or would you rather him be sick with him by your side?" I don't think there's a parent out there, who wouldn't choose to live without him, as long as he's healthy.

As much as we may hate the alienating parent, many aren't bad parents. They've got issues that have caused them to do this, and act against the child's best interest, but they still love the kid. They are still going to make sure that the kid is warm and dry and fed and healthy. There's some comfort in that.

MARIE- Thank you, Mike, for sharing your insights with everyone reading this. I applaud your work.

You can get Mike's book *A Family's Heartbreak: A Parent's Introduction to Parental Alienation* at Amazon.com. You can also visit his website at afamilysheartbreak.com.

Endnotes & Links

Links may expire over time. Updated links are available at www.MarieWhiteAuthor.com under the "Strength for Parents" tab.

1. http://www.huffingtonpost.com/megan-devine/stages-of-grief_b_4414077.html
2. https://www.competitivedge.com/why-do-some-athletes-get-sick-their-stomach-games
3. http://www.mayoclinic.org/diseases-conditions/depression/expert-answers/vitamin-b12-and-depression/faq-20058077
4. http://www.livestrong.com/article/436651-the-effects-of-sunlight-fresh-air-on-the-body/
5. http://www.depressionhealth.net/natural-therapies-to-overcome-depression/superfoods/
6. http://www.stevepavlina.com/blog/2005/07/overcoming-negative-emotions-and-boosting-motivation/
7. http://www.mayoclinic.org/healthy-lifestyle/stress-management/in-depth/stress/art-20046037
8. http://www.mayoclinic.org/diseases-conditions/depression/expert-answers/vitamin-b12-and-depression/faq-20058077
9. http://shereadstruth.com/2015/06/16/jochebed/

Copyrights Continued

Scripture taken from the New Century Version®. Copyright © 2005 by Thomas Nelson. Used by permission. All rights reserved.

Scripture quotations marked HCSB are taken from the Holman Christian Standard Bible®, Copyright © 1999, 2000, 2002, 2003, 2009 by Holman Bible Publishers. Used by permission. Holman Christian Standard Bible®, Holman CSB®, and HCSB® are federally registered trademarks of Holman Bible Publishers.

Scripture taken from the New King James Version®. Copyright © 1982 by Thomas Nelson. Used by permission. All rights reserved.

Scripture quotations marked (ESV) are from The Holy Bible, English Standard Version® (ESV®), copyright © 2001 by Crossway, a publishing ministry of Good News Publishers. Used by permission. All rights reserved.

Scripture quotations taken from the 21st Century King James Version®, copyright © 1994. Used by permission of Deuel Enterprises, Inc., Gary, SD 57237. All rights reserved.

The quotation marked (NLV) is taken from the New Life Version of the Bible by ©Christian Literature International.

NET Bible® copyright ©1996-2006 by Biblical Studies Press, L.L.C. http://netbible.com All rights reserved.

Scripture quotations marked (NLT) are taken from the Holy Bible, New Living Translation, copyright © 1996, 2004, 2007 by Tyndale House Foundation. Used by permission of Tyndale House Publishers, Inc., Carol Stream, Illinois 60188. All rights reserved.

Quotations marked GW, Scripture is taken from GOD'S WORD®, © 1995 God's Word to the Nations. Used by permission of Baker Publishing Group.

Scripture taken from The Message. Copyright © 1993, 1994, 1995, 1996, 2000, 2001, 2002. Used by permission of NavPress Publishing Group.

Scripture quotations taken from the Amplified® Bible, Copyright © 2015 by The Lockman Foundation. Used by permission.

Scripture quotations marked (GNT) are from the Good News Translation in Today's English Version-Second Edition Copyright © 1992 by American Bible Society. Used by Permission.

Scripture quotations marked (ERV) are taken from the HOLY BIBLE: EASY-TO-READ VERSION © 2014 by Bible League International. and used by permission.

Scripture from the King James Version is public domain.

*Throughout the book some names and details have been changed to protect privacy.

A Gift for You

To get your first free gift, take a selfie with this book or eBook and tag Marie on Twitter, Facebook, or Instagram.

Get a second free gift by sending this email to everyone in your email address book.

"I just read the most incredible book! It's about surviving one of life's most devastating events. I really want you to know about it and to read it for yourself. It's called *This Book is For You.*"

After sending the email take a picture of the sent screen with the date and tag the author on Facebook, Twitter, or Instagram.

Did you enjoy the book? If so, leave a review on Goodreads or Amazon because your review might give another person the gift of hope.

Hotlines

In the United Kingdom 116 123
In Australia 13 1114 or 1 300 659 467
Worldwide www.befrienders.org

Hope is a Weapon.
Survival is Victory.
—From the movie *Dunkirk*

Read about the KLOVE 30 day challenge at bit.ly/1BSsjBL and go to KLOVE.com to listen online or find a station.

Thanks

This book would not be what it is today without Logan Clarke, Ray Mitsch, Sue Cornbluth, Tim Benson, Mike Jeffries, and Bret Hohenberger.

I also want to thank Dennis J. Langais for helping me hone the title for this book.

III

Part Three

Three-hundred world-class leaders…Roosevelt and Churchill…Mahatma Ghandi and Martin Luther King…75% of them…had some serious physical disability or had been abused as children or had been raised in poverty.
—Zig Ziglar

Inspiration Cards

These cards were designed for you to cut out and place around your home, work, and vehicle. Put them in places you will see throughout the day. There were times when sticky note versions of these cards would get me through some of the toughest moments.

For eBook readers, a printable version of the cards is available at www.MarieWhiteAuthor.com.

Miracles are a retelling in small letters of the very same story which is written across the whole world in letters too large for some of us to see.

-C.S. Lewis

I rise before dawn and cry out for help; I put my hope in Your word.

Psalm 119:147 HCSB

On the day you're ready to give up

Don't give up

Don't give in

You're focusing on the trees

See the forest

For he will deliver the needy who cry out, the afflicted who have no one to help.

Psalm 72:12

Now to him who is able to do immeasurably more than all we ask or imagine, according to his power that is at work within us

Ephesians 3:20

Anger, bitterness, and hate all over promise and under deliver. Take a deep breath.
~Just breathe~

Deliver me, my God,

from the hand of the wicked,

from the grasp of those who are evil and cruel.

Psalm 71:4

Do not be far from me, my God;
come quickly, God, to help me.

Psalm 71:12

You only need
enough courage
to make it through the moment.

Those who plant in tears will harvest with
shouts of joy.

Psalm 126:5 NLT

Be strong and courageous;
don't be terrified or afraid of them. For it
is the Lord your God
who goes with you; He will not leave you
or forsake you.

Deuteronomy 31:6 HCSB

If we could see into the future
and the size of the blessing that this trial was going
to bring our way,
then we would understand
in part
the importance of the battle
we are fighting.

I would have despaired had I not believed that I
would see the goodness of the Lord in the land of
the living.

Psalm 27:13 AMP

No one who hopes in you will ever be put to shame,
but shame will come on those who are treacherous
without cause.

Psalm 25:3

Sustain me as You promised, and I will live;
do not let me be ashamed of my hope.

Psalm 119:116 HCSB

The Lord is near the brokenhearted; He saves
those crushed in spirit.

Psalm 34:18 HCSB

Be merciful to me, O God, be merciful, because
I come to you for safety. In the shadow of your
wings I find protection until the raging storms
are over.

Psalm 57:1 GNT

I prayed to the Lord, and he answered me. He
freed me from all my fears.

Psalm 34:4 GNT

This poor man cried, and the Lord heard him,
and saved him out of all his troubles.

Psalm 34:6 KJV

Do not rejoice over me, oh my enemy. Though I
have fallen, I will rise!

Micah 7:8 NIV

For I know the plans I have for you," declares the
Lord, "plans to prosper you and not to harm you,
plans to give you hope and a future.

Jeremiah 29:11

Yea, though I walk through the valley of the shadow
of death, I will fear no evil; For You are with me;
Your rod and Your staff, they comfort me.

Psalm 23:4 NKJV

I call on the Lord in my distress,

and he answers me.

Psalm 120:1

Do not be far from me, my God;
come quickly, God, to help me.

Psalm 71:12

I have told you all this so that you won't lose your
faith when you face troubles.

John 16:1 ERV

May all who want to take my life
be put to shame and confusion;
may all who desire my ruin
be turned back in disgrace.
May those who say to me, "Aha! Aha!" be appalled
at their own shame.

Psalm 40:14-15

CHAPTER 17

Daily Checklists

Week One

Daily checklist:
- o 60 minutes of sunlight
- o 30 minutes outside
- o Eat a banana
- o Avoid depressing songs/books/movies

Daily checklist:
- o 60 minutes of sunlight
- o 30 minutes outside
- o Eat a banana
- o Avoid depressing songs/books/movies

Daily checklist:
- o 60 minutes of sunlight
- o 30 minutes outside

- Eat a banana
- Avoid depressing songs/books/movies

Daily checklist:
- 60 minutes of sunlight
- 30 minutes outside
- Eat a banana
- Avoid depressing songs/books/movies

Daily checklist:
- 60 minutes of sunlight
- 30 minutes outside
- Eat a banana
- Avoid depressing songs/books/movies

Daily checklist:
- 60 minutes of sunlight
- 30 minutes outside
- Eat a banana
- Avoid depressing songs/books/movies

Daily checklist:
- 60 minutes of sunlight
- 30 minutes outside
- Eat a banana
- Avoid depressing songs/books/movies

Week Two

Put yourself on a daily laughter diet. According to the Mayo Clinic, "When you start to laugh, it doesn't just lighten your load mentally, it actually induces physical changes in your body."
Laughing increases feel-good hormones to your brain, relieves your stress response, produces a calm feeling and relaxes your muscles.

Daily checklist:
- 60 minutes of sunlight
- 30 minutes outside
- 30-60 minutes of exercise
- Banana
- Take B-complex vitamins*
- Avoid depressing songs/books/movies
- Watch something that makes you laugh

Daily checklist:
- 60 minutes of sunlight
- 30 minutes outside
- 30-60 minutes of exercise
- Banana
- Take B-complex vitamins*
- Avoid depressing songs/books/movies
- Watch something that makes you laugh

Daily checklist:
- 60 minutes of sunlight

*Always consult your doctor before starting a vitamin regimen.

- o 30 minutes outside
- o 30-60 minutes of exercise
- o Banana
- o Take B-complex vitamins*
- o Avoid depressing songs/books/movies
- o Watch something that makes you laugh

Daily checklist:
- o 60 minutes of sunlight
- o 30 minutes outside
- o 30-60 minutes of exercise
- o Banana
- o Take B-complex vitamins*
- o Avoid depressing songs/books/movies
- o Watch something that makes you laugh

Daily checklist:
- o 60 minutes of sunlight
- o 30 minutes outside
- o 30-60 minutes of exercise
- o Banana
- o Take B-complex vitamins*
- o Avoid depressing songs/books/movies
- o Watch something that makes you laugh

Daily checklist:
- o 60 minutes of sunlight
- o 30 minutes outside
- o 30-60 minutes of exercise
- o Banana
- o Take B-complex vitamins*

- Avoid depressing songs/books/movies
- Watch something that makes you laugh

Daily checklist:
- 60 minutes of sunlight
- 30 minutes outside
- 30-60 minutes of exercise
- Banana
- Take B-complex vitamins*
- Avoid depressing songs/books/movies
- Watch something that makes you laugh

Week Three

Daily checklist:
- o 60 minutes of sunlight
- o 30 minutes outside
- o Banana
- o 30-60 minutes of exercise
- o Take B-complex vitamin*
- o Avoid depressing songs/books/movies
- o Watch something that makes you laugh
- o Talk with an uplifting friend

Daily checklist:
- o 60 minutes of sunlight
- o 30 minutes outside
- o Banana
- o 30-60 minutes of exercise
- o Take B-complex vitamin*
- o Avoid depressing songs/books/movies
- o Watch something that makes you laugh
- o Talk with an uplifting friend

Daily checklist:
- o 60 minutes of sunlight
- o 30 minutes outside
- o Banana
- o 30-60 minutes of exercise
- o Take B-complex vitamin*
- o Avoid depressing songs/books/movies
- o Watch something that makes you laugh
- o Talk with an uplifting friend

Daily checklist:
- 60 minutes of sunlight
- 30 minutes outside
- Banana
- 30-60 minutes of exercise
- Take B-complex vitamin*
- Avoid depressing songs/books/movies
- Watch something that makes you laugh
- Talk with an uplifting friend

Daily checklist:
- 60 minutes of sunlight
- 30 minutes outside
- Banana
- 30-60 minutes of exercise
- Take B-complex vitamin*
- Avoid depressing songs/books/movies
- Watch something that makes you laugh
- Talk with an uplifting friend

Daily checklist:
- 60 minutes of sunlight
- 30 minutes outside
- Banana
- 30-60 minutes of exercise
- Take B-complex vitamin*
- Avoid depressing songs/books/movies
- Watch something that makes you laugh
- Talk with an uplifting friend

Daily checklist:

- 60 minutes of sunlight
- 30 minutes outside
- Banana
- 30-60 minutes of exercise
- Take B-complex vitamin*
- Avoid depressing songs/books/movies
- Watch something that makes you laugh
- Talk with an uplifting friend

Week Four

Use this week to start learning a new skill. It's as easy as taking a free class online though Udemy or YouTube. Ideally you should choose something physical like learning to rollerblade, play the guitar or painting. If you do an outside activity such as basketball, you would get your 60 minutes of sunlight, 30 minutes outside and 60 minutes of exercise, all while learning a new skill.

"Every time you learn something new, your brain changes in a pretty substantial way. In turn, this makes other parts of your life easier because the benefits of learning stretch further than just being good at something.[5]"

Daily checklist:
- o 60 minutes of sunlight
- o 30 minutes outside
- o 30-60 minutes of exercise
- o Banana
- o Take B-complex vitamin*
- o Learn a new skill

Daily checklist:
- o 60 minutes of sunlight
- o 30 minutes outside
- o 30-60 minutes of exercise
- o Banana
- o Take B-complex vitamin*
- o Learn a new skill

Daily checklist:
- 60 minutes of sunlight
- 30 minutes outside
- 30-60 minutes of exercise
- Banana
- Take B-complex vitamin*
- Learn a new skill

Daily checklist:
- 60 minutes of sunlight
- 30 minutes outside
- 30-60 minutes of exercise
- Banana
- Take B-complex vitamin*
- Learn a new skill

Daily checklist:
- 60 minutes of sunlight
- 30 minutes outside
- 30-60 minutes of exercise
- Banana
- Take B-complex vitamin*
- Learn a new skill

Daily checklist:
- 60 minutes of sunlight
- 30 minutes outside
- 30-60 minutes of exercise
- Banana
- Take B-complex vitamin*
- Learn a new skill

Daily checklist:
- 60 minutes of sunlight
- 30 minutes outside
- 30-60 minutes of exercise
- Banana
- Take B-complex vitamin*
- Learn a new skill

ABOUT THE AUTHOR

Marie White is the host of the popular YouTube series, **Bible Stories for Adults,** which has over half a million views and reaches people in every part of the world.

She is also the bestselling author of the award-winning book, *Strength for Parents of Missing Children*, a non-denominational Christian missionary, podcast host and lover of people.

To learn more about the Bible, watch her YouTube video series, **Bible Stories for Adults**.

To contact the author, visit www.MarieWhiteAuthor.com.
Instagram @MarieWhiteAuthorOfficial
Twitter @MarieWritesBook

Like what you've read? Try another of Marie's books. **Ten Day Bible Study** is available in paperback, ebook and Audible audiobook. The perfect study to do alone or with a group.

Have a little one in your life? Get a copy of Marie's children's book, *I Think of You*. "When you're tying your shoes or brushing your hair, even though I'm not there I think of you."

THIS BOOK IS FOR YOU • 193

Have you been wondering if God has abandoned you because you are LGBTQI?

Are you a Christian who wants to share the love of Jesus with your LGBTQI friends?

Are you a parent, struggling fo find a way to reach out to your LGBT teen?

With suicide, depression, domestic abuse, and drug addiction up to 400% higher in the LGBTQI community, there is a huge need to be reminded of God's love.

Take a moment to get this book and share it with a friend.

Love by another person can fade, but God's love lasts forever.

Currently used by missionaries in Greece, *Ten Day Bible Study* in modern Greek is available in both digital and print editions.

Dear friend,

I hope that by reading this book you realize that you are loved. You are not just loved by another person. You are loved by the creator of the universe. He created you with a specific purpose for your life and He can't wait for you to start living it. The first step is to invite Him into your heart. Is there anything that is keeping you from asking Jesus into your life right now?

Let's pray.

God, thank you for being so loving and kind. Thank you that You never give up on us. Thank you for sending Jesus to die a brutal death so that He could pay for every wrong thing that any human has ever done. We get to enter heaven because of what Jesus did for us.

If we wrote down every wrong thing that we have ever thought or done, it would devastate us. Our sins are too much to bear. But You said that if we confess our sins, You are faithful and just to forgive us of our sins and make us clean in Your eyes. (1 John 1:9)

Erase our sins and let us start fresh with You in our lives. Help us wipe every sinful memory from our minds and help us to remember that because we ask You to, You will make us clean.

You said that whoever hears Your words from the Bible, believes that Jesus is Your son and invites Jesus to be in their lives has passed from death into life. (John 5:24) We ask for that today. Erase our sins. Free us from hurt and bondage. Rescue us and let us have a relationship with You that is beyond anything that we could ever imagine. (1 Corinthians 2:9)

We ask all of this in the most powerful name under heaven, the name of Jesus. (Acts 4:12) Amen.

If you would like to find out more about who Jesus is, I encourage you to start reading the book of John in the New Testament section of the Bible. The New International Version (NIV) of the Bible is written in plain English and can be found in almost any store. You can also read it online at BibleGateway.com.

-Marie

When all is said and done, the life of faith is nothing if not an unending struggle of the spirit with every available weapon against the flesh.
-Dietrich Bonhoeffer

www.ingramcontent.com/pod-product-compliance
Lightning Source LLC
Chambersburg PA
CBHW020421010526
44118CB00010B/362